ALSO BY DAVID G. MYERS

NONFICTION

The Human Puzzle

The Inflated Self

Inflation, Poortalk, and the Gospel

The Human Connection

The Pursuit of Happiness

The American Paradox

A Quiet World

Intuition

Psychology Through the Eyes of Faith

What God Has Joined Together

A Friendly Letter to Skeptics and Atheists

TEXTBOOKS

Social Psychology

Psychology

Exploring Psychology

Exploring Social Psychology

Psychology in Everyday Life

Myers' Psychology for the AP Course

HOW DO
WE KNOW
OURSELVES?

HOW DO
WE KNOW
OURSELVES?

■ ■ ■

Curiosities and Marvels
of the Human Mind

DAVID G. MYERS

FARRAR, STRAUS AND GIROUX

NEW YORK

Farrar, Straus and Giroux
120 Broadway, New York 10271

Twenty-two of these essays previously appeared, in slightly different form,
on TalkPsych.com. "The Psychology of Division" was adapted from a
Politico Magazine essay titled "The Psychology of the Sunni-Shia Divide."

Grateful acknowledgment is made for permission to reprint an excerpt from *Psychology*,
13th edition, by David G. Myers and C. Nathan DeWall. Copyright © 2021 by Worth
Publishers. All rights reserved. Used by permission of the publisher Macmillan Learning.

Library of Congress Cataloging-in-Publication Data
Names: Myers, David G., author.
Title: How do we know ourselves? : curiosities and marvels of the human mind / David G.
  Myers.
Description: First edition. | New York : Farrar, Straus and Giroux, [2022] | Includes
  bibliographical references. |
Identifiers: LCCN 2022023782 | ISBN 9780374601959 (hardcover)
Subjects: LCSH: Psychology.
Classification: LCC BF149 .M94 2022 | DDC 150—dc23/eng/20220711
LC record available at https://lccn.loc.gov/2022023782

Designed by Gretchen Achilles

Our books may be purchased in bulk for promotional, educational,
or business use. Please contact your local bookseller or the Macmillan Corporate
and Premium Sales Department at 1-800-221-7945, extension 5442, or by email at
MacmillanSpecialMarkets@macmillan.com.

www.fsgbooks.com
www.twitter.com/fsgbooks · www.facebook.com/fsgbooks

For Carol,
my companion on the journey of life

CONTENTS

PART II: WHO ARE WE?

PART III: WHAT IN THE WORLD?

PREFACE

As a researcher and professor of psychological science, I am animated by two aims: to enable people, amid a sea of misinformation, to think smarter about their lives, and to help them savor the wonders within and around us.

I've been privileged to pursue these aims over five decades by teaching and by writing textbooks for psychology students worldwide. I am fortunate to be charged with harvesting the first fruits of my discipline, to file new research in my office cubbyholes nearly every day, and then to distill and give away the newsworthy insights.

Reading my discipline's discoveries leaves me sometimes surprised, occasionally awestruck, and frequently fascinated by the human mind. Often I encounter some new discovery or insight and think, "This is something educated people need to know!" Over the years I've written in-depth books for general readers on topics ranging from the scientific pursuit of happiness to the powers (and perils) of intuition. Here I instead share a wide-ranging assortment of psychological science findings.

Some of the musings that follow were sparked by new research that illuminates some facet of our lives. Others occurred spontaneously as I witnessed human events and saw a psychological science explanation. Thus were born these reflections on the marvels of our minds. Some appear here for the first time; many are adapted from musings originally published on my *Talk Psych Blog*.

The essays appear in three clusters: "Who Am I?" (focusing on the self); "Who Are We?" (exploring our relationships); and "What in the World?" (taking a psychological eye to the larger world around us).

I offer this book hoping that you—or someone you know—might enjoy these short and sometimes playful glimpses of psychology's wisdom. Or perhaps, having already studied psychology, you might welcome a recap and an update of its mind-expanding offerings.

The essays all aim to shine the light of psychological science on our sometimes bewildering and ever-fascinating lives. Each has a simple premise: although we all know a lot, we don't know what we don't know—even about ourselves.

PART I

■

WHO AM I?

1

IMPLICIT EGOTISM

You surely know why you chose your town, your partner, and your vocation—all for good reasons, no doubt.

But might other, unknown reasons—operating beneath your awareness—also have nudged your choices? This is the implication of *implicit egotism*—an automatic tendency to like things we associate with ourselves. For example, we come to like familiar things, including our own familiar face. Thus, we prefer a politician or stranger who looks like us—indeed, whose face has been morphed with some features of our own.

We also find someone more *attractive* when our face has been morphed with theirs. "Facial resemblance is a cue of kinship," noted the University of Glasgow researcher Lisa De-Bruine, who earlier had also found more trust of people with "self-resembling same-sex faces." I can relate, having once been conned out of $20 by a seemingly desperate person seeking a taxi fare who I later reflected looked rather like me. Implicit biases operate behind the scenes.

I see you yawning: "You needed research to know that

we love ourselves and things that resemble us?" The surprise comes with the many ways this phenomenon has been documented.

One example is the *name-letter effect*. People of varied nationalities, languages, and ages prefer the letters that appear in their own name. People also tend to marry someone whose first or last name resembles their own.

A second is the *birth date–number effect*. People likewise prefer the numbers that appear in their birth date. In one experiment, people, after having their self-concept challenged by briefly thinking about their weaknesses, "were more attracted than usual" to other people whose laboratory participant number (such as 11–22) resembled their own birth date.

Or consider the *name-residence effect*. Philadelphia, having many more people than Jacksonville, has had (no surprise) 2.2 times more men named Jack . . . but also *10.4* times more named Philip. Ditto Virginia Beach, which has a disproportionate number of women named Virginia, and St. Louis, which, compared with the national average, has 49 percent more men named Louis. Likewise, folks named Park, Hill, Beach, Rock, or Lake are disproportionately likely to live in cities (for example, Park City) that include their surnames.

If that last finding—offered by the social psychologist Brett Pelham and his colleagues—doesn't surprise you, consider an even weirder phenomenon they uncovered: people seem to gravitate to careers identified with their names. In the United States, Dennis, Jerry, and Walter have been equally popular names. But dentists have twice as often been named Dennis as Jerry or Walter, and two and a half times more often named Denise than the equally popular Beverly or Tammy. Among geoscientists (geologists, geophysicists, and geochemists), people named George and Geoffrey are similarly overrepresented.

The phenomenon extends to *surname-occupation matching*. In 1940 U.S. Census data, people named Baker, Barber, Butcher, and Butler (and seven other occupations that double as names) were all more likely than expected—sometimes much more likely—to work in occupations associated with their names.

Ah, but do Pelham and his colleagues have cause and effect reversed? Uri Simonsohn, a behavioral scientist with a knack for exposing questionable findings, has argued exactly that. For example, aren't towns and streets often named after people whose descendants stick around? And are people in Virginia more likely to name girls with the state name? Are Georgians more likely to christen their babies Georgia or George? Wasn't the long-ago village baker—thus so named—likely to have descendants carrying on the ancestral work?

Likely so, grants Pelham. But could that, he asks, explain why states have an excess of people sharing a last-name similarity? California, for example, has an excess of people whose names begin with Cali (as in Califano). Moreover, he reports, people are more likely to *move* to states and cities with name resemblances—Virginia to Virginia and Tex to Texas, for example.

I thought of this playful surname-occupation research when reading a paper on the cognition of black bears, co-authored by Michael Beran. Next up in my reading pile was creative work on problem-solving by crows, led by Chris Bird. Soon after, I was reading about interventions for lifting youth out of depression, pioneered by Sally Merry.

That took my delighted mind to the important books on animal behavior by Robin Fox and Lionel Tiger, and to the *Birds of North America* volume by Chandler Robbins.

The list goes on: the billionaire Marc Rich, the drummer Billy Drummond, Ronald Reagan's White House spokesman Larry Speakes.

Internet sources offer lots more: dentists named E. Z. Filler, Gargle, and Toothaker; the Oregon banking firm led by Cheatham and Steele; and the chorister Justin Tune. But as an internet meme reminds us, "The problem with quotes on the Internet is that you never know if they're true" (Abraham Lincoln).

Perhaps you, too, have some favorite name-vocation associations? I think of my good friend who was anxious before meeting his oncologist, Dr. Bury. (I am happy to report that two decades later my friend is robustly unburied and did not need the services of the nearby Posthumus Funeral Home.) Another friend recalled that his parents' hot water heater was installed by two men named Plumber and Leak.

If our implicit egotism unconsciously influences our preferences, might that explain why it was Susie who sold seashells by the seashore?

Although the phenomenon is usually only a modest influence on our preferences, it does introduce us to a larger reality: the surprising scale and power of the unseen implicit mind. In ways Freud never anticipated, our preferences, perceptions, memories, and attitudes operate on two levels—a conscious, deliberate "high road" and a much larger yet invisible "low road" where the mind works below the radar of our awareness.

Reflecting on this vast out-of-sight information processing, the great cognitive psychologist George Miller once described two ocean liner passengers gazing over the sea. "There sure is a lot of water in the ocean," said one. "Yes," replied the other, "and we've only seen the top of it."

2

THE AMAZING POWER OF ATTENTION

Like a flashlight beam, our mind's selective attention focuses at any moment on but a small slice of our experience. It's a phenomenon most drivers underestimate when distracted by phone texting or conversation. And unlike the modest implicit egotism phenomenon, the riveting of our single-minded attention is huge.

Magicians are masters at attention manipulating—thus leaving unnoticed their hand slipping into the pocket while our attention is misdirected elsewhere. As the mind-messing magician Teller has said, "Every time you perform a magic trick, you're engaging in experimental psychology."

Understanding the phenomenon does not confer immunity to it. One Swedish psychologist, after being surprised by a woman exposing herself on a Stockholm street, later realized he had been outwitted by pickpocketing thieves, who understood the focusing power of his selective attention.

Among the many weird and wonderful (and now familiar) perceptual phenomena is our blindness to things right in front of our eyes. In famous demonstrations of *inattentional blindness*, people who were focused on a task, such as counting the number of times black-shirted people pass a ball, often failed to notice a woman with an umbrella sauntering through the scene. In other mischievous experiments, it was a person in a gorilla suit or a clown on a unicycle who went undetected in plain sight.

This looking-without-seeing phenomenon illustrates a deep truth: *Our attention is powerfully selective. Conscious awareness resides in one place at a time.* When we attend to one thing, we necessarily ignore all else. Attention is a finite resource.

That much you likely already knew. What's less well known is how this selective inattention restrains other senses, too. *Inattentional deafness* is easily demonstrated with "dichotic listening" tasks. The researchers pipe novel tunes into a person's one ear while they focus on to-be-repeated-out-loud words fed into their other ear. The surprising result: afterward, they won't be able to identify what tune they have just heard. Their attention was focused elsewhere. (Thanks to a "mere exposure effect," they will, however, later *like* the unperceived tune better than other similar novel tunes.)

In an acoustic replication of the invisible gorilla study, the University of London psychologists Polly Dalton and Nick Fraenkel asked people to focus on a conversation between two women (rather than on two men who were simultaneously talking). Selective inattention resulted: the participants usually failed to notice one of the men repeatedly saying, "I am a gorilla."

A recent British experiment further documents *inattentional numbness*. Pickpockets have long understood that bumping into people makes them unlikely to notice a hand slipping into their pocket. Dalton (working with Sandra Murphy) experimented with this tactile inattention. Sure enough, when distracted, her participants failed to notice an otherwise easily noticed vibration to their hand.

Tactile inattention sometimes works to our benefit. Once, while driving to give a talk, I experienced a painful stabbing in my eye (from a torn contact lens) . . . then experienced no pain while giving the talk . . . then felt the excruciating pain again on the drive home. In clinical settings, such as with patients receiving burn treatments, distraction can similarly make painful procedures tolerable. Pain is most keenly felt when attended to.

Another British experiment, this one by Sophie Forster and Charles Spence, demonstrated *inattentional anosmia*, an inability to smell. When participants focused on a cognitively demanding task, they were unlikely to notice a coffee scent in the room.

So what's next? Can we expect a demonstration of inattentional *ageusia*? ("Ageusia": an inability to taste—my new word for the day.) Surely, given our powers of attention (and corresponding inattention), we should expect it.

The moral of this story—that our attention is a wonderful gift, given to just one thing at a time—is but one small example of the marvels of our mind. The more neuroscientists learn, the more convinced they are that what is truly extraordinary is not supposed extrasensory perception, claims for which have not survived investigation, but rather our everyday sensory-perceptual system.

Consider: as you read these words, light energy particles strike your retinal receptor cells, which convert them into neural signals that activate adjacent cells, which process the information for a third cell layer, from which emerges a nerve tract that shoots electrochemical messages up to your brain, where, step by step, what you are viewing is reassembled into its component features and then somehow composed into a consciously perceived image, which is instantly compared with previously stored information and recognized as words you know.

The process is rather like taking a house apart, transporting its elements to a different location, and then, through the work of millions of specialized workers, reconstructing it—and in but a fraction of a second. Moreover, this effortless, implicit information processing transpires continuously, in motion, in three dimensions, and in color.

The deeper one explores these very ordinary things of life, the more one empathizes with Job: "I have uttered what I did not understand, things too wonderful for me." Things extraordinary lie within the ordinary.

Sherlock Holmes understood: "It is a mistake to confound strangeness with mystery. The most commonplace crime is often the most mysterious . . . Life is infinitely stranger than anything which the [human mind] could invent."

3

THERE IS MORE TO HEARING THAN MEETS THE EARS

At a National Institute on Deafness and Other Communication Disorders advisory council meeting, I was surprised to hear one of its executives repeatedly emphasize the institute's "missionaries." Who are these missionaries, I wondered—ambassadors for hearing health? On about the fifth utterance I recomputed: *mission areas!*

Like vision, hearing is both *bottom-up* (as our inner ear transforms sound waves into neural messages) and *top-down* (as our brain imposes meaning on the neural input). In an effortless microsecond, our brain transforms the blizzard of sensations into a conscious perception. Listening to our language—sounds created from an unparsed string of air pressure waves—our brain instantly carves out distinct words. Lacking ear lids, we can't help it.

But sometimes, in its hunger to find order and form in sensory input, our brain gets it wrong. So it was when the writer Sylvia Wright, while a child, misperceived a Scottish ballad—

"They hae slaine the Earl of Murray, And hae laid him on the green"—as "They hae slain the Earl of Murray, and *Lady Mondegreen.*" And so was born the term "mondegreen"— meaning a misheard phrase or word.

Mondegreens have two parents: inexperience and context. Thanks to their inexperience with language and with life in general, children have been a fount of mondegreens, as when singing, "Lo, in the gravy lay, Jesus my Savior." Even as an adult, I can recall bemusement when hearing a choir's "You who unto Jesus" as "Yoo-hoo unto Jesus." Music lovers have recorded thousands of mondegreens at www.kissthisguy.com, a website named for the mishearing of the guitarist/singer Jimi Hendrix's phrase "kiss the sky." Thus, OneRepublic's "too late to apologize" gets heard as "too late to order fries," Madonna's "Like a virgin touched for the very first time" is received as "for the thirty-first time," and Eurythmics' "Sweet dreams are made of this" becomes "Sweet dreams are made of cheese."

Context shapes auditory perceptions. While listening to sad rather than happy music, report Jamin Halberstadt and colleagues, people tend to perceive homophone words with a sad meaning—"mourning" rather than "morning," "die" rather than "dye," "pain" rather than "pane." Context similarly gives birth to mondegreens by creating expectations (perceptual sets). Depending on our perceptual set, we may hear "rhapsody" or "rap city," "sects" or "sex," "meteorologist" or "meaty urologist."

Mondegreens are pervasive in computer voice translation. I asked my iPhone Siri, "What is a mondegreen?" and it responded "What is Mom the green?" Microsoft's speech recognition group used to call itself the "Wreck a Nice Beach" group—because their task was to "recognize speech."

Mondegreens are an occasional experience for normal-hearing people. But for those of us with hearing loss—people who hear sound but struggle to carve meaning from it—mondegreens are commonplace. The former *Hearing Health* editor Paula Bonillas recalls giving her daughter castanets for Christmas, when actually her daughter had hoped for a casting net. I recall my wife telling me of her picture of "an autumn scene" and my puzzled reaction that she would enjoy a picture of "an autopsy."

As the physicist Paul Davies and I discussed our hearing loss recently, he recalled his visit to a Sydney, Australia, beach. A woman emerged from the men's bathroom he was approaching. "Had sex today?" she cheerfully seemed to ask. As the speechless Davies fumbled for an answer, he realized that the women's bathroom was broken, so she was explaining herself by saying the men's bathroom was "unisex today."

Much as Norwegians can tell Norwegian jokes to one another, those of us in the hearing loss community laugh knowingly at our mishearings, and even at our in-jokes, such as about the three golfers with hearing loss. "It's windy," remarks one. "No, says the second, it's Thursday." "Me, too," says the third. "Let's go get a drink."

Sometimes the results of our mishearings are not trivial, as when the kindly airline pilot, during takeoff, told his depressed co-pilot, "Cheer up." The co-pilot heard the expected "Gear up" and raised the wheels—before they had left the ground. The co-pilot would get empathy from the hard-of-hearing person who, driving on a rainy night and about to pull out into traffic, heard her companion's "No!" as "Go!" . . . and rammed into a passing car. A bad hear day.

Our everyday struggle to discern meaningful speech amid noise reminds us of a deep lesson: We are automatic meaning makers. Our minds are adept pattern seekers. Shown random markings, we may see a face on the moon, the Madonna on a pizza, or an illusory figure, such as this nonexistent triangle:

As visual illusions and mondegreens demonstrate, much of what we perceive comes from behind our eyes and between our ears. *We perceive reality not exactly as it is but as our brains interpret it.*

And lest we take it for granted, let's pause to marvel at that sensing, pattern-finding, meaning-making hunk of tissue. By itself, floating in its skull-encased inner world, the brain feels nothing, sees nothing, hears nothing. And yet, fed information from external sensors, its pulsating network of some 128 billion neurons somehow makes mind. It constructs our perceptions of a campfire's heat, flicker, scent, and crackle.

It guides our motions, acquires our skills, and drives our reproduction. It enables us to experience elation, remember our grandmother, and plan our future—all while automatically monitoring and maintaining our body's operation. The psalmist's poetry discerned rightly: we are "fearfully and wonderfully made."

4

HOW DO WE KNOW OURSELVES?

We know ourselves partly by observing our own actions, proposed the Cornell University social psychologist Daryl Bem. Bem's self-perception theory assumed that our behavior is often self-revealing. We observe our actions, then infer our attitudes. Hearing ourselves talk can clue us to our sentiments. Witnessing our actions gives us insight into the strength of our convictions (much as we observe others' behavior and make inferences).

The limits of such self-revelation have been explored by a creative research team at Sweden's Lund University. Andreas Lind and his colleagues were curious: If you said one thing, but heard yourself saying another, what would you think you said? Would you believe what your mouth said or what your ears heard come out of your mouth?

The researchers experimented. Through a headset, their participants first heard themselves correctly name various *font colors*, as when saying "gray" when the word "green" appeared in a gray font. But then the wily researchers sometimes inserted a participant's previously recorded voice saying an incorrect word, such as "green." Surprisingly, what people heard usually controlled their perception of what they had actually said. On two-thirds of the trials, people experienced the inserted word (in their own voice) as self-produced!

The self-revealing power of our behavior also appears in the *facial feedback effect*. Psychologists have confirmed this self-perception effect by inducing people to make a frowning expression—by asking them to pull their brows together and contract certain muscles, supposedly to enable the attaching of facial electrodes. Voilà! Doing so triggers a small twinge of anger. Likewise, a manipulated smiling expression leads people to feel happier and to find cartoons funnier.

You can experience this, too. Scowl. Then fake a hearty grin. Can you feel a smile therapy effect? Even holding a pencil in the lips, which activates smiling muscles, feels happier than holding a pencil with the teeth. To be sure, we frown when we're sad, scowl when we're angry, and smile when we're happy. But we also feel sadder when frowning, angrier when scowling, and happier when smiling. Let Botox paralyze your facial muscles associated with a sad or happy emotion and you will feel less of the emotion.

At Germany's University of Cologne, the psychologist Sascha Topolinski and his colleagues report that even subtle word articulation movements of the mouth come tinged with emotion. In nine experiments, they invited both German- and English-speaking people to silently read nonsense words and names spoken with inward (swallowing-like) mouth movements—for example, "BENOKA"—or outward (spitting-like) movements, such as "KENOBA." The consistent result: people prefer the words associated with ingesting movements. Likewise, supposed chat partners given names (such as Manero) that activated ingestion muscles were preferred over partners whose names activated muscles associated with spitting (such as Gasepa).

The pioneering American philosopher and psychologist William James, who struggled with depression, observed that we can tweak our emotions by going "through the outward movements" of whatever emotion we wish to experience. "To feel cheerful, sit up cheerfully . . . and act as if cheerfulness were already there." Charles Darwin similarly noted that outwardly expressing an emotion "intensifies it." You can experience this "*behavior* feedback effect." Do like the participants in one experiment: Take a walk with short, shuffling steps and eyes downcast. Then shift to long strides with arms swinging and eyes straight ahead. Can you feel the difference?

In a University of Alberta experiment, Gary Wells and Richard Petty invited students to "test headphone sets" by making either horizontal or vertical head motions while listening to an opinion piece. Those making the nodding vertical movements later were more likely to say they agreed with the opinion they had heard. Motions affect emotions. To be—and feel—agreeable when talking with someone, nod your head.

In another experiment, led by the late John Cacioppo, American psychology students rated neutral stimuli (unfamiliar Chinese ideograph characters) more positively when pressing their arms *upward* against a table (as when lifting food or celebrating a triumph) than they did when pressing them downward (as when pushing someone or something away). The positive associations of upward flexion infused the stimuli with more positive overtones. (Can you feel a subtle emotional difference while lifting a table edge with upturned hands rather than pressing down on it?)

The self-perception phenomenon can increase our empathy for others. To experience others' feelings, we can consciously mirror their expressions and synchronize our movements with theirs. To some extent, we do this naturally, and the result is *emotional contagion*. We mimic another's action, and then feel what they feel. Those who lose this mimicry ability—such as when experiencing facial paralysis—find it harder to reflect back, and even feel, others' happiness or sadness.

The self-perception principle is simple: our expressions and actions are self-revealing. Sometimes we observe ourselves and infer our thoughts and feelings. "Self-knowledge," said Goethe, "is best learned not by contemplation, but by action."

5

DUAL PROCESSING:
ONE BRAIN, TWO MINDS?

O ne of the stunning, believe-it-or-not revelations of psychological science concerns how much more we know than we know we know. We operate with, so to speak, two minds—one conscious, and the other larger and out of sight, below the radar of our awareness. We have one brain with two tracks, each supported by its own neural equipment. We call it dual processing.

Yes, Freud long ago distinguished between the conscious and the unconscious minds. But today's understanding of the out-of-sight mind is not Freud's seething unconsciousness, with its repressed sexual and aggressive urges. It's a cooler and bigger information processing system.

Our memory, thinking, language, attitudes, and perceptions all operate on these two tracks—a conscious, deliberate "high road" and an unconscious, automatic "low road." Our high-road mind is reflective; our low-road mind is intuitive.

Consider driving: Your brain and hands know how to

move into the right lane. But if you are like most drivers, you can't consciously explain how you do it. Most drivers say they would bank right, then straighten out. But that would steer them off the road. Actually, after moving right, you reverse the steering wheel equally to the left of center, and only then return to the center position. But no worries, your low-road-guided hands know how to do it.

The same is true of a tennis player's response to an oncoming serve, a batter's response to a low-and-inside fast pitch, or a basketball player's in-motion body instantly calculating the physics of an off-balance shot—all of which happen too instantly for conscious control. The moral: our brain is a device for transforming conscious into unconscious knowledge.

Two striking phenomena—*blindsight* and *implicit memory*—illustrate our dual minds, each with who-would-have-guessed findings.

Blindsight: A stranger-than-fiction true story: During a sabbatical and subsequent visits to Scotland's University of St. Andrews, I became acquainted with the cognitive neuroscientists David Milner and Melvyn Goodale. They studied a local woman, D.F. (keeping her name confidential), who had suffered carbon-monoxide-caused brain damage that left her unable to recognize and discriminate objects by sight. Consciously, she could see nothing.

Yet she exhibited blindsight. She *behaved* as though she could see. Given a postcard to slip into a vertical or horizontal mail slot, she could not see the mail slot, yet, when coaxed to try, she could slip the postcard into the slot. Asked to estimate the width of a small block held in front of her, she was clueless. Yet she could reach out and grasp it with the right finger-thumb distance.

How could she do this? Don't we all have one visual system?

From animal research, Milner and Goodale knew that the eyes send information simultaneously to different brain areas to work on different subtasks such as discerning motion, form, depth, and color (a related phenomenon we call parallel processing). And sure enough, D.F.'s brain activity revealed damage in the area concerned with consciously recognizing objects, but normal activity in the area that underlies reaching, grasping, and navigating around objects.

How strange and wonderful is this thing called vision, explain Milner and Goodale in their book *Sight Unseen*. Our vision is not the single system we presume. It is, instead, a dual processing system that operates simultaneously on a *visual perception track* that enables us "to think about the world" (to recognize objects and plan our actions) and a *visual action track*—"a zombie within"—that guides our movements.

Blindsight has similarly been observed in other patients, and even in those of us with intact brains. Disable the cortex of normally sighted people with magnetic stimulation and they will still be able to guess the nature of unseen stimuli. Or, via goggles, show people's left and right eyes different scenes, perhaps a dog to the left eye and a cat to the right eye. One scene will dominate: we can be aware of only one thing at a time. Nonetheless, people display some blindsight awareness of the unperceived scene (such as by guessing the location of a probe stimulus within it).

Researchers have also used magnetic stimulation to deactivate people's sense of touch, leaving them unaware of where someone has touched them. Yet, like some patients who have suffered sensory cortex damage, they can display a blindsight-like *numbsense*—by guessing the touch location. The unconscious mind knows what the conscious mind does not.

Implicit memory: Our memory likewise operates on two tracks, each with its own neural underpinnings. Your brain's centrally located hippocampus and its frontal lobes are processing sites for your *explicit* (conscious) memories. If you lost those areas, you would, however, still be capable of recording *implicit* (unconscious) memories for skills and for newly conditioned associations.

My father was one such person. A brain bleed at age ninety-two left him unable to form new conscious memories. Told of his brother-in-law's death, he expressed surprise and sadness each time he received the news. After I would answer his question about our dinner plans, he might, fifteen minutes later, ask again (and again) about our dinner plans. Yet such people can learn nonverbal tasks. Shown hidden figures in *Where's Waldo?* pictures, they can quickly spot them again. They can find their way to the bathroom, though without being able to tell you where it is.

The neuroscientist Joseph LeDoux recounted a brain-damaged patient whose amnesia meant she could not recognize her physician each day when he reintroduced himself and shook her hand. One day, after the physician had previously pricked her with a tack in his palm, she refused the handshake. After yanking her hand back, she was unable to explain why she'd done so. Having been conditioned, she implicitly remembered what she could not explicitly remember. Our memory is more than we're aware of.

The classic memory case is Henry Molaison (H.M., as he was known until his 2008 death at age eighty-two). After the removal of much of his hippocampus to control severe seizures, Molaison retained his intelligence and could remember his presurgery past. But he could not form new memories. As the neuroscientist Suzanne Corkin reported, "I've known H.M. since 1962, and he still doesn't know who I am."

The neurologist Oliver Sacks described a similar patient, Jimmie, who, after a 1945 brain injury, had no memories, and thus no sense of elapsed time. Sacks gave Jimmie a back-to-the-future experience by showing him a photograph from *National Geographic* and asking what it was.

"It's the moon," Jimmie answered.

No, Sacks explained. "It's a picture of the earth taken from the moon."

"Doc, you're kidding! Someone would've had to get a camera up there!"

"Naturally."

"Hell! You're joking—how the hell would you do that?"

Nevertheless, patients like H.M. and Jimmie can learn "procedural" skills, such as how to read mirror-image writing, do a jigsaw puzzle, or even perform certain job tasks. Yet they have no awareness of having learned such skills. "Well, this is strange," said Molaison, after demonstrating mirror tracing he had forgotten he had learned. "I thought that would be difficult. But it seems as though I've done it quite well."

Alzheimer's patients, too, may lose explicit memory for new people and events, yet retain implicit memories for new automatic skills. They can learn *how* to do something, yet have no conscious recall of what they've learned.

As with vision and memory, so also with other cognitive realms, including our explicit and implicit attitudes (as in the well-known studies of conscious prejudice and implicit bias). Although the conscious mind is disposed to believe that its intentions rule our lives, the reality of the two-track brain is otherwise. Most of our thinking, feeling, and acting operates effortlessly, outside our conscious awareness. Some "80 to 90 percent of what we do is unconscious," says the Nobel laureate and memory researcher Eric Kandel.

The upshot: our one brain houses two minds, two information processing systems. At corporate Tesla, most activity, necessarily, happens below the level of Elon Musk's awareness, which focuses on highest-priority matters. Likewise, and thankfully, most of what sustains us is done by our unseen mind operating effortlessly, without demanding our conscious mind's attention.

6

MAKING NEW YEAR'S
RESOLUTIONS THAT LAST

write at a new year transition, the line between our last year's self and our hoped-for healthier, happier, and more productive self to come. To become that new self, we know what to do. We *know* that a full night's sleep boosts our alertness, energy, and mood. We *know* that exercise lessens depression and anxiety, sculpts our bodies, and strengthens our hearts and minds. We *know* that what we put into our bodies—junk food or balanced nutrition, addictive substances or clean air—affects our health and longevity.

Alas, as T. S. Eliot foresaw, "Between the idea and the reality . . . Falls the Shadow." So how, this year, can we move from *knowing* the needed behaviors to *doing* them? How can we set goals and make them last?

Psychological science offers six strategies.

1. *Make that New Year's resolution.* Research by Gary Latham, Edwin Locke, and others confirms that chal-

lenging goals motivate achievement. Specific, measurable, realistic goals—such as "finish the business plan by the month's end"—direct attention, promote effort, motivate persistence, and stimulate creativity.

2. *Announce the goal to friends or family.* We're more likely to follow through after making a public commitment. Tell your social media friends.

3. *Develop an implementation plan*—an action strategy that specifies when, where, and how you will march toward achieving your goal. Research shows that people who flesh out goals with detailed plans become more focused in their work and more likely to complete it on time. Through the ups and downs of goal striving, we best sustain our motivation when we focus on immediate subgoals. Better to have our nose to the grindstone than our eye on the ultimate prize. Better to attend to daily study than to focus on the course grade. Better to center on small steps— the day's running target—than to fantasize about the marathon.

4. *Monitor and record progress*, perhaps aided by a tracker such as a Fitbit. It's all the better when that progress is displayed publicly rather than kept secret. Let your social media friends cheer you on.

5. *Create a supportive environment.* When trying to eat healthy, keep junk food out of the cupboards. Use small plates and bowls. When focusing on a project, hole up in the library. When sleeping, stash the smartphone. Choose the right friends. Such "situational self-control

strategies" prevent tempting impulses, Angela Duckworth and her colleagues have found.

6. *Transform the hard-to-do behavior into a must-do habit.* Habits form when we repeat behaviors in a given context—sleeping in the same comfy position, walking the same route to work, eating the same breakfast oatmeal. As our behavior becomes linked with the context, our next experience of that context evokes our habitual response. Studies find that when our willpower is depleted, as when we're mentally fatigued, we fall back on our habits—good or bad. To increase our self-control, to connect our resolutions with positive outcomes, the key is forming beneficial habits. "If you would make anything a habit, do it," said the Stoic philosopher Epictetus. As the *New York Times* writer Jane Coaston explained after managing her weight with a daily habit of recording her eating and exercising, "Now, I don't think too much about . . . walking 10,000 steps a day. I just do it."

But how long does it take to form a beneficial habit? A University College London research team led by Phillippa Lally asked ninety-six university students to choose some healthy behavior, such as eating fruit with lunch or running before dinner, and to perform it daily for eighty-four days. The students also logged whether the behavior felt automatic (something they did without thinking and would find it hard not to do). When did the behaviors turn into habits? On average, after about sixty-six days.

There's also an efficiency to the mindlessness of habits. My wife loves me, despite smirking that I am "boringly predictable." Every day, I go to bed at pretty much the same time, rise at the same time, pull on my khaki pants, frequent the same coffee shops on given days, ride the same old bicycle, and exercise every weekday noon hour. But—there is an upside to this—I have also loved the same woman for half a century, been guided by the same textbook editor for thirty-four years, and professed psychology at the same college for fifty-five years.

And there is more upside. As my colleagues and friends Roy Baumeister, Julia Exline, Nathan DeWall, and others have documented, self-controlled decision making is like a muscle. It temporarily weakens after an exertion (a phenomenon called ego depletion) and replenishes with rest. Although experiments on ego depletion have produced inconsistent results, it does seem that exercising willpower can temporarily deplete the mental energy needed for self-control on other tasks.

President Barack Obama appreciated this. As he explained to the *Vanity Fair* writer Michael Lewis, "You'll see I wear only gray or blue suits. I'm trying to pare down decisions. I don't want to make decisions about what I'm eating or wearing. Because I have too many other decisions to make." Lewis reports that Obama mentioned "research that shows the simple act of making decisions degrades one's ability to make further decisions," noting that Obama added, "You need to focus your decision-making energy. You need to routinize yourself. You can't be going through the day distracted by trivia."

So, amid today's applause for "mindfulness," let's put in a word for mindlessness. Mindless, habitual living frees our minds to work on important things. As the philosopher Alfred North Whitehead argued, "Civilization advances by extending the number of operations which we can perform without thinking about them."

7

THE POWERS AND PERILS
OF INTUITION

As a research psychologist, I have spent the last half century exploring the relationships between feelings and facts, between intuition and reality, between subjective and objective truth. I celebrate out-of-the-blue hunches and creative inspirations. Having lacked the self-confidence to date while in high school, I took an instant liking to a new college classmate, to whom I have been married since age twenty. When I meet job applicants, my gut sense of the person kicks in within seconds.

I am not alone. "Buried deep within each and every one of us, there is an instinctive, heart-felt awareness" that can guide our behavior. So proclaimed Prince Charles in a 2000 lecture. Trust your gut instincts.

"I'm a gut player. I rely on my instincts," explained President George W. Bush in justifying his decision to launch the Iraq war, after earlier talking with Vladimir Putin and declaring himself "able to get a sense of his soul."

"Don't try to comprehend with your mind," advised Madeleine L'Engle (*A Wind in the Door*). "Use your intuition." As the French philosopher Blaise Pascal observed in his 1670 *Pensées*, "The heart has its reasons which reason does not know."

But there is also wisdom to the physicist Richard Feynman's channeling the skepticism of King Solomon's proverb: "He that trusteth in his own heart is a fool." "The first principle," said Feynman, "is that you must not fool yourself—and you are the easiest person to fool."

Indeed, my own intuition often errs. I have misjudged job applicants. I am chagrined at money I've lost by trusting untrustworthy people. Even my geographic intuition—which tells me that Reno is east of Los Angeles, that Atlanta is east of Detroit, that Rome is south of New York—is wrong, wrong, and wrong.

In sifting intuition's powers and perils, psychological science has some wisdom.

First, our out-of-sight, automatic, intuitive information processing is massive. Some examples:

Automatic processing: We glide through life mostly on autopilot. Our information processing is primarily implicit, unconscious, behind the scenes. Though we would be hard-pressed to explain how we do it, we unconsciously know how to form the word "bad" rather than "pad" or that "a big red barn" sounds better than "a red big barn." When making instant judgments—friend or foe?—we use "fast and frugal" heuristics, which are mental shortcuts.

Intuitive expertise: After mastering driving, chess, or basketball jump shots, people can react to situations intuitively, without rational analysis. Learning to drive at first takes effortful concentration. But soon it becomes an intuitive skill that, while we converse, our hands and feet manage. Experienced chess masters, mechanics, and basketball point guards can often read and respond to a situation with but a glance.

Blindsight: Some blind people, as we noted earlier, display an astonishing "blindsight"; they can, for example, intuitively place an envelope in a mail slot they cannot consciously see. Without their knowing how they do it, their unseen sight guides their hand.

Reading others: We are skilled at reading "thin slices" of behavior—as when judging someone's warmth from a six-second video clip. Viewing but ten seconds of a professor's teaching will make you a reasonably accurate judge of the professor's enthusiasm and energy. Even a micro-thin-fraction-of-a-second glimpse of a face or object can trigger an emotional response. "We're finding that everything is evaluated as good or bad within a quarter second," reported the Yale social psychologist John Bargh from his studies on the automaticity of everyday life.

Our intuitive genius is pretty amazing, especially given that we share 90 percent of our DNA with a cow. But as Pascal long ago taught us, any truth separated from its complementary truth is a half-truth. Intuition is power, but it also is perilous. Psychology is flush with examples of smart people's predictable and sometimes tragic intuitive errors.

Human lie detection: In experiments, people barely surpass chance when intuiting whether others are lying or telling the truth. (American presidents might want to remember this when judging Putin's or Kim Jong Un's believability.) I turned this phenomenon into one of my favorite class demonstrations, by inviting ten students to draw a slip that instructed them either to "make up a lie" or to "tell the truth" about some past experience. Inevitably, the other class members would greatly overestimate their ability to discern which was which.

Intuitive prejudice: As demonstrated in some police responses to ambiguous situations, implicit biases can—without any conscious malevolent intent—affect our perceptions and reactions. (Is that man pulling out a gun or a phone?) The "prejudice habit"—manifest as an instant, implicit wariness of someone unfamiliar or dissimilar—is often reflexive and hard to break.

Intuitive fears: We fear things that kill people vividly and memorably (because we intuitively judge risks by how readily images of a threat come to mind). Thus, we may—stay tuned for more to come on this—fear flying more than driving, shark attacks more than drowning, school mass shootings more than street and home shootings.

The "interview illusion": Given our ability to read warmth from thin slices, it's understandable that employment interviewers routinely overestimate their ability to predict future job success from unstructured get-acquainted interviews. But aptitude tests, work samples, job-knowledge tests, and peer ratings of past job performance are all better predictors. Even the lengthiest of interviews—the mate-selection process—is a fragile predictor of long-term marital success.

Moreover, consider: If "heart, intuition, guts" provide a

wise guide to investors, as so many believe, then why aren't stock market day traders or savvy mutual fund executives able to outguess the efficient marketplace (which, as the Princeton economist Burton Malkiel has shown, they cannot)? If gamblers—*any* gamblers—have a valid gut instinct, then why are there not more than the expected winners of Powerball mega lotteries? And if some psychics—*any* psychic—had intuitive powers of foreseeing the future, reading minds, and viewing remote happenings, then why were none able to claim the magician James Randi's long-standing million-dollar prize to the first who could do so? As the skeptic Michael Shermer has noted, if such psychic intuitions were commonplace, then there would be no surprise parties, hands of "rock, paper, scissors" would end in a draw, and hide-and-seek would be a short, dull game. But alas, investors', gamblers', and psychics' intuitions are the stuff of fools.

The bottom line: Intuition—automatic, implicit, unreasoned thoughts and feelings—grows from our experience, feeds our creativity, and guides our lives. Intuition is powerful. When restrained by the data of hard reality, intuition can ignite achievement. But when unchecked, intuition is perilous, especially when we overfeel and underthink. Uncritical intuition sometimes, alas, leads us into ill-fated relationships, feeds overconfident predictions, and even steers us into war. The heart has its reasons, but the rational mind often thinks smarter.

8

FEARING THE RIGHT THINGS

We humans have a puzzling tendency to fear the wrong things. We routinely display *probability neglect* by fretting about vividly publicized remote possibilities while ignoring higher probabilities. Dramatic catastrophes make us gasp, while statistical probabilities we barely grasp.

Thus, we may fear airline flights more than driving, though over the last decade driving has been, per mile traveled, 501 times more likely to kill us. In a late 2020 Gallup World Poll of more than a hundred thousand people, 39 percent of those over sixty-five were understandably "worried about their health under COVID." But among those eighteen to twenty-nine, despite having more than a hundredfold lower death risk, a similar 40 percent expressed COVID fears (an exaggerated fear that served a positive purpose—of self-protection that restrained community spread). And how many parents agonize about statistically rare terrorist acts, school shootings, and child abductions . . . while not bothering to strap their child into a car seat?

My granddaughter's elementary school experienced a lock-down after a "creepy-looking guy" (without a gun) entered the district's adjacent high school building and followed a girl into a bathroom. Police cars swarmed the area, helicopters flew overhead, and eventually the frightened children were ushered onto their home-going buses under the gaze of officers with semiautomatic weapons.

Such exaggerated fears of school terror were completely understandable after promise-filled lives were lost in the horrors of Parkland and Columbine and Newtown. So, yes, schools and law enforcement *should* prepare for the possibility of copycat violence.

But whatever makes national news and captures our attention is, by definition, something that rarely happens—and thus something that, though horrific, is actually less to be feared than the undramatic, ongoing threats that claim lives one by one, as in the more than forty thousand lives taken each year (one hundred and twenty per day) by suicidal, homicidal, and accidental gun deaths.

As psychology students know well, our fears are fed by the *availability heuristic*—our tendency to estimate the commonality of events based on their mental availability. Whatever information pops readily into mind—often vivid, recent, distinctive images—can seem more frequent (and dangerous) than it actually is. And what is more vivid than those scenes from Marjory Stoneman Douglas High School?

When statistically infrequent (but traumatizing) incidents of air crashes, domestic terrorism, and school shootings hijack our consciousness—thanks to our heuristic of judging risk by readily available images of horrific happenings—we will disproportionately fear such things. For example, Gallup reports that nearly half of Americans (38 percent of men and 58 percent of women) now are "worried" that they or a family member will be a mass shooting victim.

Feeling such fear, we may allocate scarce public resources in less-than-optimal ways—as when transforming schools into fortresses with frightened children—while being unconcerned about the vastly greater dangers posed by car accidents and guns in the home. Guns kill more than forty thousand Americans a year. Among the victims are more children than die of cancer. Yet the Harvard risk expert David Ropeik calculates that the likelihood of any given student being killed by a gun in school on any given day is incomprehensibly small—1 in 614 million—"far lower than almost any other mortality risk a kid faces, including traveling to and from school" or playing sports. Moreover, student safety has increased thanks to a dramatic drop from 1993 to 2019 in students who acknowledge bringing a gun, knife, or club to school (from 12 to 3 percent).

A second, lesser-known fear-producing mechanism is *border bias*. We categorize events as pertinent to us (or not) partly by whether they happen in "our" state or country. Two places seem closer and more vulnerable to the same natural disaster, such as a tornado, if labeled as in the same state—rather than as in equally distant places in adjacent states.

The United States is a vast country. But its being one country enables people in the Pacific Northwest (where my granddaughter's school lockdown occurred) to identify with people in farthest-away southern Florida . . . even if, with 140,000 U.S. schools, any given child's vulnerability to a school shooting is considerably less than that of a traffic fatality. (In one recent year, 2,829 teens died in motor vehicle crashes.)

If, like Europe's Belgium, the Netherlands, and France, our geography was categorized into different countries, would we be less fearful after tragic events happening "in other countries"? As in the experiments, would the boundaries of our mental maps affect our perceived risk?

While taking prudent measures to protect children, could we—mindful of how availability and border bias hijack our thinking—better align our fears (of diseases, climate threats, guns, and accidents) with reality? "If the Stoneman Douglas shooting is finally going to stir Americans' consciences about the unique violence of childhood here, let's make sure that the discussion doesn't end with guns," wrote David Leonhardt. As an example, he argued for "'graduated drivers licenses,' in which teenagers slowly gain privileges as they gain experience . . . The goal, after all, should be saving lives."

Leonhardt's point, and mine, is not that we should be unperturbed by school shootings, but rather this: if we really care about minimizing tragedy and suffering, we should not let our anguished feelings hijack our thinking. Next to the evil and emotions of a school shooting (or being eaten by a shark), "statistics seem cold and irrelevant," acknowledged Ropeik. But, he argued, exaggerated fears of an "extraordinarily rare risk," as dramatized for my granddaughter, do their own form of harm to children's security and well-being.

Ergo, let's focus not on the last bad thing but on actual

risks associated with everything from guns to climate change. Numbers matter because the real risks to lives everywhere matter—for those we know and with whom we empathize, and those unseen and in the future, for whom it is so difficult to feel empathy.

9

WE KNEW IT ALL ALONG

I t's one of psychology's underappreciated lessons: *anything seems obvious, once it happens.* After the stock market drops, we recognize that it was "due for a correction." After the football game, we credit a winning coach for a "gutsy" game-ending play and fault a losing coach for the same "stupid play." After an election, its outcome seems predictable. How easily we presume that we knew and know more than we did and do.

We call this phenomenon *hindsight bias* (a.k.a. the "I knew it all along" phenomenon). As the philosopher Søren Kierkegaard recognized, "Life is lived forwards, but understood backwards."

Demonstrating hindsight bias is easy. Give someone a purported psychological finding, and give someone else an opposite result. The first person might read, "Social psychologists have found that we are most attracted to people whose traits are similar to our own. As the old saying goes, 'Birds of a feather flock together.'"

1. In a sentence, why do you suppose this is?
2. Do you find this result ___ surprising ___ unsurprising?

Have the other person read an opposite finding: "We are most attracted to people whose traits differ from our own. As the old saying goes, 'Opposites attract.'"

I have done this demonstration many times in classes, by giving half the class each result. Regardless of whether I tell students the truth (similarity → attraction) or its opposite, my repeated experience is that nearly all will raise hands to indicate that their finding is unsurprising. They knew it all along.

As the demonstration suggests, we can draw on proverbs to make sense of many a plausible result. If we find that separation intensifies romantic attraction, people may roll their eyes: "You get paid for this? My grandmother could have told you that 'absence makes the heart grow fonder.'" Should it turn out that separation weakens attraction, Mr. Public will scorn, "Well, duh. 'Out of sight, out of mind.'"

Proverbs are typically short and memorable, noted the Norwegian researcher Karl Teigen, but may be contradictory. Consider: Do "too many cooks spoil the broth" or "many hands make light work"? Should we "keep our eye on the prize" or "our nose to the grindstone"? Can we not "teach an old dog new tricks," or are we "never too old to learn"? Is "he who hesitates lost," or should we "look before we leap"?

Teigen must have had a few laughs after asking students to evaluate actual proverbs and their opposites. Told "Fear is stronger than love," most rated it as true. But so did students who were given its reversed form, "Love is stronger than fear." Likewise, the genuine proverb "He that is fallen cannot help him who is down" was rated highly, but so too was "He that is fallen can help him who is down." But my favorites were the authentic proverb "Wise men make proverbs and fools repeat them" and its made-up counterpart, "Fools make proverbs and wise men repeat them."

The point of the phenomenon, which has been observed in more than eight hundred investigations in people young and old from around the world, is not that common sense is usually wrong. Rather, common sense describes, after the fact, what *has* happened better than it predicts what will happen. As the physicist Niels Bohr reportedly jested, "Prediction is very difficult, especially about the future."

The phenomenon can make psychological science findings seem like common sense. Once people learn a research result, and explain it, the outcome seems predictable—much less surprising than to those simply told about the research and its possible outcomes, and especially those asked to imagine and explain an opposite result. Indeed, you perhaps now are thinking that you knew this all along?

Duke University's Center for Advanced Hindsight appreciates the phenomenon's power. The center, its website declares,

> was created out of our love affair with the hindsight bias, a phenomenon where people find things to be more predictable after they have occurred. This bias is

particularly interesting in behavioral science research, where we often hear that our research results are intuitive. But we only hear that they are intuitive if people don't have to guess beforehand what happened in an experiment. When we ask people to guess the results beforehand, we find they are quite poor at predicting (and therefore the results of the research are not so intuitive after all!).

Hindsight bias also has a way of making history seem like a series of inevitable events, when in actuality the future is seldom foreseen. No one's diary recorded, "Today the Hundred Years' War began."

Thus, after the 9/11 attack, investigators found signals that made the disaster seem obvious: A U.S. Senate investigative report listed the missed or misinterpreted clues. The CIA knew that al-Qaeda operatives had entered the country. An FBI memo warned headquarters of "the possibility of a coordinated effort by Osama bin Laden to send students to the United States to attend civilian aviation universities and colleges." The president had received a briefing titled "Bin Ladin Determined to Strike in US" and remained on vacation.

But what seems clear in hindsight ("What malfeasance not to have seen this coming!") is seldom clear on the front side of history. In the six years before 9/11, the FBI's counterterrorism unit could hardly have pursued all sixty-eight thousand uninvestigated leads, though, in hindsight, the few useful ones became obvious. Nevertheless, because outcomes, once known, seem predictable, we tend to blame decision makers for what are in retrospect "obvious" bad choices and not to praise them for good choices, which also seem "obvious." *After* the sudden and chaotic collapse of the Afghan government, pundits (who never predicted such) disparaged President Joe Biden for not having foreseen it.

Moreover, we blame not only others for "stupid mistakes" but also ourselves. Looking back, we realize how we should have handled a person or a situation. "I should have known how busy I would be and started that project earlier." "I should have realized sooner that he was not to be trusted." "I should have known not to risk money on that stock." But sometimes we are too hard on ourselves. We forget that what is obvious to us now was not nearly so obvious at the time.

As Sherlock said to Dr. Watson, "It is easy to be wise after the event."

10

JUDGING OTHERS AND JUDGING OURSELVES

As we pull down controversial statues and reassess historical figures," let's also examine our own moral blind spots, urged the *New York Times* journalist Nicholas Kristof. Although our moral failings may not be on the horrific scale of those who enslaved their fellow humans, we likely still have what Kristof called "moral myopia." Kristof suggested three possible contenders for such blind spots: the animal cruelty of factory farming, indifference to suffering in impoverished countries, and climate change. He anticipated that a century from now, future generations may judge our actions in these areas as "bewilderingly immoral."

Many of us can already look back on events in our own lives with embarrassment. I recall reveling, with other Pacific Northwesterners fifty-five years ago, in the first killer whale captures. Today, we understand those captures as a brutal separation of orcas from their family and a contribution to the

endangered status of our region's beloved seventy-four southern resident orcas. And might morally enlightened future
people want to remove my name from something for attitudes or actions I have more recently embraced—perhaps for
eating the flesh of animals, or for flying on climate-destroying
aircraft? Perhaps even for attitudes and behaviors I am now
too shortsighted to imagine as problematic to my descendants? When judging the speck in someone else's eye, do I
fail to notice what is in my own?

An oft-demonstrated truth is that most of us have a great
reputation with ourselves and therefore may miss the large
specks in our own lives. Psychologists, as I will elaborate later,
call this the *self-serving bias*. We accept more responsibility
for our good deeds than for our bad. And we tend to see
ourselves as better than average—as more honest, as more
charitable, and as decidedly more moral than others.

This self-serving bias can lead us to view ourselves as morally superior to our ancestors. We presume that had we stood
in their shoes, we would have behaved differently. We are
like the people who—when told about experiments in which
people have conformed to falsehoods, followed orders to administer painful shocks, or failed to help someone—predict
that *they* would have acted more truthfully and courageously.
But psychology's experiments have indicated otherwise.

The Princeton legal scholar Robert George tweeted that
he sometimes asks students "what their position on slavery would have been had they been white and living in the
South before abolition. Guess what? They all would have

been abolitionists! They all would have bravely spoken out against slavery, and worked tirelessly against it." But this is "nonsense," he adds. Had we been white southerners, embedded in that time and culture's systemic racism, most of us would likely have been, to a lesser or greater extent, complicit. He challenges those who think they would have been the exception to tell him how they have, in their current life, done something similarly unpopular with their peers, causing them to be abandoned by friends and "loathed and ridiculed by powerful, influential individuals and institutions."

Of course, a brave minority in the South did join the abolitionist cause and enabled the Underground Railway. And under Hitler a few brave souls did resist, protest, and suffer.

But such heroes are heroes because they are the exception. Experiments show that most people do err when confidently predicting that they would intervene where others have not if witnessing a sexist or racist slur. In one experiment, Janet Swim and Lauri Hyers invited Penn State University students to imagine themselves in a small group discussing whom to select for survival on a desert island. How would they imagine themselves reacting to a man injecting sexist comments such as "I think we need more women on the island to keep the men satisfied"? (How would *you* react?)

Only 5 percent predicted they would ignore the sexist remarks or wait to see how others responded. But when other students were actually in a situation where a man made these comments, 55 percent—not 5 percent—said nothing.

Likewise, most folks predict they would be upset when hearing a racial slur and would respond accordingly. But people actually experiencing this typically exhibit indifference. T. S. Eliot's words ring true again: "Between the idea and the reality . . . Falls the Shadow."

11

BEHAVIORAL CONFIRMATION: GETTING WHAT WE EXPECT

Picture the setting: In a University of Minnesota lab, a male student talks on the phone with a woman he believes, from a photograph he's been shown, is either strikingly attractive or unattractive. The woman—who is clueless of the man's misimpressions—proceeds to speak more warmly to the man if he thinks she's attractive.

Did you catch what happened in this clever experiment with fifty-one undergraduate pairs by the social psychologist Mark Snyder and his colleagues? The men's beliefs were self-fulfilling—a phenomenon that Snyder called *behavioral confirmation*. Thinking a woman attractive (or unattractive) led the men to act in a way that induced the women to reciprocate the men's attraction (or not).

The phenomenon can be overstated (studies indicate that self-fulfilling prophecies have "less than extraordinary power"). Yet there is evidence that teachers' expectations of students, parents' expectations of children, and managers' expectations of workers are sometimes self-confirming. In experiments, those led to believe they are liked behave more warmly and, in return, *are* liked more. Interviewees whom an interviewer expected to be warm behaved more warmly. And men believed to be sexist have been led to treat women less favorably.

The effect has also been observed with children. After measuring the amount of classroom litter, Richard Miller and his co-researchers had the teacher tell one class they should be neat and tidy. That temporarily increased the amount of trash placed in wastebaskets from 15 to 45 percent. Another class was instead, over eight days, congratulated for being neat and tidy, which led these children to increase their trash deposits from 15 to 80 percent. Likewise, when told they are hardworking and kind, children have become more likely to live up to those labels.

So, would close relationships flourish when partners idealize each other? Are positive illusions self-fulfilling? Or, as sometimes happens, do they more often create unrealizable, self-defeating expectations? More the former, reported the psychologist Sandra Murray from her studies of dating couples. Idealization buffered conflicts and helped transform frogs into princes or princesses. When someone loves and admires you, it helps you become that person.

The same phenomenon has been observed among married couples. When you expect a partner to be in a good, loving mood, you likely will behave more warmly—thus eliciting the expected mood. Those who expect the worst of their partner—who presume the partner doesn't accept and love them—are prone to then interpret slights as rejections.

In response, they will further devalue the partner and emotionally distance themselves. Those who instead assume their partner's love and goodwill tend to read less into stressful events and to respond less defensively. Love helps create its reality.

Behavioral confirmation also appears in laboratory games, because hostility begets hostility. If one believes an opponent will be uncooperative, the opponent typically responds by becoming so. Each side's believing that the other is resentful and vindictive will trigger the other to behave accordingly in self-defense, thus creating a vicious circle. Similarly, nations may exhibit mirror-image perceptions that assume the worst of another nation: "We are peace loving, but they are treacherous." The result is sometimes an arms race, or even war.

And so it happens in everyday life, sometimes with a negative result: Jill, presuming Jack is annoyed, snubs him, which leads Jack to respond curtly, thus confirming her presumption.

The simple lesson: What we see in others may get reflected back in how they react to us. And what others see in us may influence how we respond to them. Our social beliefs both reflect and create our social reality. As we expect, so we shall find.

12

HOW DO I LOVE ME?
LET ME COUNT THE WAYS

The great counseling psychologist Carl Rogers once objected to the religious doctrine that humanity's problems arise from excessive self-love—a.k.a. pride, the foundation of the seven deadly sins. In his experience, most people instead "despise themselves, regard themselves as worthless and unlovable." As the comedian Groucho Marx once jested, "I wouldn't want to belong to any club that would accept me as a member."

Actually, most of us have a good reputation with ourselves. In studies of self-esteem, even those who score relatively low will fall in the midrange of possible scores. Responding to statements such as "I have good ideas" or "I am fun to be with" with a middling "somewhat" or "sometimes" will mark you as having *low* self-esteem. In every one of fifty-three countries studied, the average self-esteem score was above the midpoint of the scale's range of possible scores.

High self-esteem scores are but the first pointer to one of

psychology's most provocative, life-relevant, and oft-replicated findings: we humans commonly exhibit *self-serving bias*. We perceive ourselves as better than most and explain events in self-enhancing ways. If that doesn't surprise you (Rogers's belief notwithstanding), consider how this phenomenon lurks in the human psyche, starting with the better-than-average phenomenon.

The sixth-century B.C. Chinese philosopher Lao-tzu said that someone "who is sane [will never] over-reach himself, over-spend himself, over-rate himself." If so, then nearly all of us are a little insane.

Name any subjective and socially desirable dimension—intelligence, looks, health, tolerance, insightfulness, job competence, morality, and so on—and I will guarantee you that most people will see themselves as better than the average person.

The humorist Dave Barry had that idea: "The one thing that unites all human beings, regardless of age, gender, religion, economic status, or ethnic background, is that, deep down inside, we all believe that we are above-average drivers." Indeed, drivers—even most drivers who have been hospitalized in accidents—believe themselves to be safer and more skilled than the average driver.

A sampling of other research findings:

Competence: In surveys, 90 percent of business managers have rated their performance as superior to that of their average peer. The same is true of college instructors, more than 90 percent of whom have rated their teaching as better than average. Eighty-six percent of Australians rated their job performance as above average; only 1 percent rated their performance as below average. And most surgeons believed their patients' mortality is lower than average. When merit raises are distributed, many workers will surely feel mistreated with an average or even below-average reward. And when most people in a group believe they are underpaid and underappreciated, given their "better-than-average" contributions, disharmony and envy will surely result.

Ethics and virtues: "How would you rate your own morals and values on a scale from 1 to 100 (100 being perfect)?" In a national survey, 50 percent of respondents rated themselves 90 or higher; only 11 percent said 74 or below. Thus, most American businesspeople saw themselves as more ethical than the average businessperson. Most Dutch high school students rated themselves as more honest, persistent, reliable, and friendly than their average peer. And most folks saw themselves as more likely than others to give to charity, give up their bus seat to a pregnant woman, or donate blood. University students reported they are more likely (90 percent) than their peers (75 percent) to vote in an upcoming election, although only 69 percent actually did. (Their predictions of others' behavior were more accurate than their self-predictions.)

Health: Most people viewed themselves as healthier than most of their neighbors. And most college students believed they would outlive the actuarial prediction of their age of death by ten years—a finding that Freud foresaw in his reputed joke about the husband who told his wife, "If one of us dies, I shall move to Paris."

Attractiveness: Is it your experience, as it is mine, that most photographs of you don't quite do you justice? One clever experiment showed people several faces—one their own, the others being their face morphed with those of less and more attractive faces. Asked which was their own real face, most folks identified an attractively enhanced version of their actual face.

Effort: As a general rule, group members' estimates of what fraction of the effort they contribute to a joint task will usually sum to more than 100 percent. In a survey of heterosexual married partners, 49 percent of husbands estimated that they did half to most of the childcare, while only 31 percent of their wives agreed. And while 56 percent of the husbands said *they* do most of the cooking, 70 percent of the wives said *they* did.

My wife and I used to pitch our dirty laundry each night on the floor next to our clothes hamper. The next morning, one of us would move the clothes into the hamper. When she suggested I not leave this mundane task to her, I thought, "What? I already do it 75 percent of the time!" So I asked how often she thought she picked up the clothes. "Oh," she replied, "about 75 percent of the time." And we wonder why some happy honeymooners mature into aggrieved spouses?

Social skills: I first stumbled across the better-than-average phenomenon when noting a peculiar result buried in a College Board survey of 829,000 high school seniors. Asked to rate themselves in "ability to get along with others," almost *none* (less than one-half of 1 percent) rated themselves below average. Sixty percent rated themselves in the top 10 percent. And 25 percent put themselves in the top 1 percent.

So, we all live in Garrison Keillor's fictional Lake

Wobegon—where "all the women are strong, all the men are good-looking, and all the children are above average." The Lake Wobegon effect, as I have called it, is strongest for traits that are not just socially desirable but also subjective: for social skill more than for math ability; for honesty more than running speed; for leadership skill more than singing ability.

We not only tend to see ourselves as better than most; we also explain good and bad events in ways that protect or enhance our self-regard. "Victory finds a hundred fathers but defeat is an orphan," wrote the Italian diplomat Count Galeazzo Ciano, words later echoed by John F. Kennedy. That's an apt summary of many dozens of experiments. In each, people have accepted credit when informed they've succeeded, attributing their success to their effort and ability. But when told they've failed, they attribute the result to something external—perhaps bad luck or the "impossible" task.

In real-life settings, athletes credit themselves for victories and more often attribute losses to bad breaks, bad refereeing, or the other team's exceptional performance or dirty play. And those better-than-average drivers? On insurance forms, they have explained accidents as "An invisible car came out of nowhere, struck my car, and vanished," or "As I reached an intersection, a hedge sprang up, obscuring my vision, and I did not see the other car," or even "A pedestrian hit me and went under my car."

Students similarly sustain their positive self-understanding by accepting responsibility for successes and verbally distancing themselves from failures. "I got an A on my psych test," but "The professor gave me a C on my lit essay."

Situations that blend chance and skill are made-to-order conditions for these self-serving attributions. When I win at Scrabble, it's confirmation of my vast verbal reservoir. When I lose, it's because "Who could do anything with a *Q* but no *U*?"

So, when business profits soar, CEOs welcome large bonuses for leading their companies to success. And when their companies lose money, well, "It's what one would expect in a down market."

Self-serving attributions feed bargaining impasses, worker-management disputes, and marital disagreements. While managers often blame disappointing results on workers' inability or indolence, the workers will more often attribute the underperformance to poor management or an excessive workload. And it likely will not surprise you to know that divorced people usually attribute most of their marital problems to their partner.

To some extent, self-serving bias is a natural result of how we observe and process information. I could more easily picture myself putting the dirty clothes in the hamper than all the times I didn't. And my wife, too, was surely more likely to notice and recall her own actions than mine. But our biased perceptions also reflect our self-enhancing emotions. As much research shows, we're not just cool information-processing computers; we're motivated to find self-affirmation—to boost our self-image. Given a generic description of our personality based on a test or even our astrological sign, we're likely to find it credible—when it is favorable. Flattery feels factual.

Ironically, this bias is so potent that, as the Princeton social psychologist Emily Pronin observed, people's "bias blind spot" even leads them *to think themselves less vulnerable than average to self-serving bias*, which they more readily see in others. In politics as in relationships, others, we agree, are biased, but we are more objective. We are not so different from the Pharisee who prayed, "God, I thank you that I am not like other people."

I hear you objecting, "But I often hear people putting themselves down, and I sometimes feel inferior myself." Indeed, all of us some of the time feel inferior when comparing ourselves with those a step or two higher on the ladder of looks, grades, or income. And some of us much of the time—notably those suffering from depression—do not exhibit self-serving bias. In experiments, depressed folks do not see themselves as better than average or shirk responsibility for failure. They are, in the words of one prominent researcher, "sadder but wiser"—a phenomenon that clinical researchers call "depressive realism."

Self-serving bias is social psychology's modern story of pride. Although pride often goes before a fall, there's adaptive wisdom in moderate self-serving bias. Some self-disparagement can be subtly self-serving. Putting ourselves down can elicit reassuring words from friends: "I wish I weren't so ugly" may elicit "Oh, come now, you're so cute."

Believing in our relative superiority also emboldens us to venture and potentially succeed where others fear to go. The opposite—doubting our relative competence and social skill, and blaming setbacks on ourselves—undercuts our potential for leadership or success.

Even so, self-serving pride is often perilous. In a debate with Carl Rogers, the theologian Reinhold Niebuhr argued that humanity's original sin—its fundamental flaw—is excessive self-love, pretension, and pride. Self-serving pride leads us to disparage one another. The flip side of assuming credit for our individual and group achievements is blaming the seemingly less deserving poor for their poverty and the oppressed for their oppression. Pride fuels racism, sexism, nationalism, and all the chauvinisms that lead one group of people to see themselves as more able, more deserving, and more moral than another.

In one of his eighteenth-century sermons, Samuel Johnson recognized the phenomenon: "He that overvalues himself will undervalue others, and he that undervalues others will oppress them."

PART II

WHO ARE WE?

13

THE SCIENCE OF HUMILITY

In today's contentious and polarized world, we struggle to reconcile the virtues of conviction and humility.

Our convictions define what matters to us. We anchor ourselves in core beliefs and values that guide our lives. Our convictions motivate our advocacy for a better world. They give us courage to speak and act. "We must always take sides," said the Holocaust survivor Elie Wiesel. "Silence encourages the tormentor, never the tormented." "To be silent is to be complicit," added Sister Helen Prejean in her 1993 book, *Dead Man Walking*.

We need deep-rooted convictions to fuel our passions. But in our age—in which, for example, the percentage of both Republicans and Democrats who "hate" the other party has soared from 20 percent in 2000 to near 50 percent in 2016—we need *humility* even more. Conviction abounds, but humility is in short supply.

Intellectual humility—knowing that one might be wrong—restrains bullheaded fanaticism. Humility enables civil discourse. Humility underlies science. Humility facilitates critical thinking, which puts testable ideas—including one's own—to the test. *Nullius in verba* (Britain's Royal Society motto): Take nobody's word for it. To accept everything is to be gullible; to deny everything is to be a cynic.

Humility also supports healthy relationships. Humility's opposite is pride, which so often feeds contempt for others. Even Dale Carnegie, America's twentieth-century positive thinking apostle, foresaw the danger: "Each nation feels superior to other nations. That breeds patriotism—and wars."

Psychology has long explored the powers and perils of pride. We have documented the following:

- *Self-serving bias.* We tend, as we've noted, to see ourselves as better than most others. And we willingly accept responsibility for our successes and good deeds while shifting the blame elsewhere for our failures and misdeeds.
- *Cognitive conceit.* We tend to display excessive confidence in the accuracy of our judgments and beliefs.
- *Unrealistic optimism.* University students perceive themselves as much more likely than their peers to get a good job, own a house, and draw a good salary, and as much less likely to develop an alcohol problem, get fired, or suffer a heart attack by middle age. Newlyweds think themselves immune to the fate of 40 percent of marriages—divorce.

Humility, by contrast, entails *an accurate understanding of self.* To paraphrase C. S. Lewis, true humility is not thinking we are less than others, but rather allows us to recognize both our own talents and others' strengths. Humility also involves *modest self-presentation*. When we share and accept credit without seeking attention, we are not (to again paraphrase C. S. Lewis) thinking less of ourselves but thinking of ourselves less. Last, when we are humble, we have *an orientation toward others*. Prioritizing others' needs helps us regulate our own impulses. With a spirit of humility we can engage others with the anticipation that, on some matters, the other is our superior—thus giving us an opportunity to learn.

True humility can be distinguished from pseudo-humility, which comes to us in two forms. One is the *pretense* of humility. Someone who says "I am humbled to accept this award . . . to serve as your president . . . to have scored the winning goal" is actually proud of their accomplishment—and deservedly so.

The other form was demonstrated by Ovul Sezer, Francesca Gino, and Michael Norton in their research on the humblebrag. Humblebragging is boasting disguised as complaining or humility: "I've got to stop saying yes to every interview request." "I can't believe I was the one who got the job over three hundred other applicants!" "No makeup and I still get hit on!" But such self-promotion usually backfires, they report. People often see through the humblebrag. It comes across as insincere and fails to elicit sympathy, convey humility, or impress others.

Other psychological studies confirm that good lives and healthy cultures are animated by convictions that are refined by humility. Humility is pro-social. It opens us to others, enriches our understandings, and builds bridges across our divides. Show social psychologists a situation where humility abounds—with accurate self-awareness plus modest self-presentation plus a focus on others—and they will show you friendship bonds and happy marriages. Where there is humility, there is the possibility of forgiveness, of smooth group relationships, and of acceptance of diversity.

Humility is also strategic. As I write these essays, I confess to savoring my own words—to taking joy in creating the flow of ideas, playing with the phrasing, fine-tuning the product to seeming perfection. *This time*, I have repeatedly told myself, my editors will find nothing to improve upon. But *always* they find glitches, holes, ambiguities, or infelicities to which I was blind.

Perhaps that is your story, too? Your best work, when reviewed by others . . . your best tentative decisions, when assessed by your peers . . . your best plans, when critiqued by consultants . . . turn into something better than you, working solo, could have created. Humility works. The pack is greater than the wolf.

Of course, there is an irony to self-assessed humility, which can lead us to feel proud of our better-than-average humility, as in Donald Trump's tweet: "The new Pope is a humble man, very much like me, which probably explains why I like him so much!"

"True humility does not know that it is humble," observed Martin Luther. "If it did, it would be proud from the contemplation of so fine a future."

So, how can we deepen our humility? C. S. Lewis had an idea: "If anyone would like to acquire humility, I can, I think, tell him the first step. The first step is to realize that one is proud. And a biggish step, too." And the second step, continued Lewis (foretelling psychological research to come), is to compare upward. Compare yourself with those wiser, shrewder, or stronger, rather than with those less so. The ultimate upward comparison, he added, is to glimpse the greatness of God and to see oneself in light of that—enabling you to "be humble, delightedly humble, feeling the infinite relief" of having let go of the pretensions that have "made you restless and unhappy."

14

WHEN BIRTH ORDER MATTERS

B irth order powerfully influences who you are, whom you marry, the job you choose, and the kind of parent you are." So proclaimed marketing for *The Birth Order Book: Why You Are the Way You Are*. This popular belief, reinforced by other books such as *The Birth Order Effect* and visible on more than three million websites mentioning "birth order," resonates with many people's experience.

Being the firstborn or middle born or "baby" in your family, you probably, from observing your siblings and yourself, have witnessed a birth-order effect. Those firstborn, it's widely believed, tend to be more domineering, conscientious, and high achieving. Those later born are more likely to be risk-taking daredevils, comedians, or even revolutionary thinkers such as Darwin and Copernicus.

It makes sense, given what the personality theorist Alfred Adler recognized long ago—that first- and later-born children have different experiences growing up in the same family. Firstborn children, for example, get more parental attention (think of all those baby book photos), while the later born often have a more permissive upbringing. No wonder firstborns have been consistently overrepresented among Harvard's first-year students (of whom they typically are 40 percent, versus the 30 percent who are youngest children).

But research offers a surprise. Despite these anecdotal observations, what most people believe about birth order isn't true.

Whether driving, gambling, adventuring, or taking paper-and-pencil tests, later-born people, studies find, are no more likely to take risks. Moreover, in big data sets and when controlling for other factors such as age, family income, and gender, firstborn individuals do not differ from the later born in conscientiousness or any of the other "Big Five" personality traits such as extraversion. They do average, perhaps thanks to that extra parental attention, a point or two higher in IQ scores, but not enough to make a noticeable difference within a family.

The birth-order effect thus joins the list of psychology's "zombie ideas"—repeatedly refuted ideas that refuse to die (for example, that we repress painful memories; that children, being fragile, should be protected from stress; that teaching should align with individual students' learning styles).

Why, then, do so many people see and believe in a birth-order effect? First, we fail to consider that birth order is confounded with family size. Small families—which have tended to be richer and more educated families—have a higher proportion of firstborn (including only) children. Later-born children more often come from larger, poorer, and less educated families, which are also less likely to send their kids to

Harvard. Birth-order effects have therefore tended to evaporate after controlling for family size.

Also, as the late Judith Rich Harris argued, birth-order differences seen within the family context—such as the oldest brother or sister being more domineering—do not generalize to nonfamily social contexts. The big brother or sister who bosses the younger siblings may not be similarly bossy in the office context.

Yet there is one amazingly reliable who-would-have-guessed-it birth-order effect that has been observed in thirty-five of thirty-six samples from multiple cultures. *Men with older brothers are somewhat more likely to be gay.* In studies by Ray Blanchard and Anthony Bogaert, the odds of same-sex attraction have been roughly 2 percent among first sons, 2.6 percent among second sons, 3.5 percent for third sons, and so forth.

This "fraternal birth-order effect" (a.k.a. the older brother effect) does not occur among women with older sisters. It also only occurs with biological (not adoptive) siblings, whether raised together or not. That strongly suggests that the cause lies with prenatal biology, not with rearing—with nature, not nurture. As the COVID-19 pandemic reminded us, the body defends itself from foreign invasions by producing antibodies. Blanchard and his colleagues surmise that male-specific proteins produced by male fetuses stimulate antibody production by the mother's immune system. And just as a second vaccine dose may boost the defensive immune response, so also with each succeeding male-fetus pregnancy: the maternal antibodies may grow stronger and affect male-typical fetal brain development.

Bogaert and his colleagues have now confirmed this maternal immune explanation in mothers of gay and straight men by measuring their level of antibodies that react to the presence of male proteins. Bogaert reports that mothers of gay sons—especially those with older brothers—had significantly higher levels of the antibody. Moreover, "these antibodies increase in concentration with each gestation of a male foetus."

This fraternal birth-order effect converges with other biological predictors of sexual orientation (prenatal hormones, genetics, and brain differences) in indicating that sexual orientation (men's, especially) is something we do not choose and cannot change. Sexual orientation is a natural, enduring disposition. Telling people otherwise has been the source of much anguish, depression, and suicide, and many failed marriages. Small wonder that so many of yesterday's "ex-gay" ministry leaders are now "ex-ex-gays."

To sum up, although birth order affects how growing-up siblings relate to one another, it has no discernible influence on adult personality. The commonplace idea that a child's birth order *does* have enduring effects jells with the larger "nurture assumption"—that parent-child interactions shape the hardening clay of one's personality development.

The extremes of parent-child relationships do matter. In Romania of the 1970s and 1980s, after years of the dictator Nicolae Ceaușescu's birth-promoting policies (outlawing contraception and abortion and taxing childless people), infants flooded into underfinanced orphanages. After Ceaușescu's fall, infants adopted out of wretched confinement thrived, while their left-behind crib mates sadly languished. So abuse and neglect leave marks. Yet within the normal range of caring parenting, children's development is more demonstrably influenced by their genes and prenatal biology and by their peers.

You perhaps object: Haven't we learned that, for example, aggressive, punitive parents tend to have more aggressive children than do gentle parents? Indeed, grants Judith Rich Harris. But those children also are born with their parents' genes. Thus, she says, comparing children from different homes is like "comparing foxhounds reared in kennels with poodles reared in apartments." Moreover, she contends, nature has prepared us to play, mate, and partner with our peers. Thus, after infancy, children and youth attend to and align more with their peers than with their parents. For example, children who hear English spoken with one accent by parents and another by friends and classmates (think of a family moving from rural Georgia to Boston) will—you can depend on this—grow up talking like their peers, not their parents.

Such findings raise perhaps psychology's biggest question (see chapter 28): How do nature and nurture form us?

15

CARDIAC ARREST AND THE CONSCIOUS EXPERIENCE OF DEATH

D eath is reversible." So began Sam Parnia, NYU Medical Center's director of Critical Care and Resuscitation Research, at a research consultation on death experiences during and after cardiac resuscitation.

Biologically speaking, he explained, death and cardiac arrest are synonymous. When the heart stops, a person will stop breathing, and within two to twenty seconds the brain will stop functioning. These are the criteria for declaring someone dead. When there's no heartbeat, no breathing, and no discernible brain activity, the attending physician records the time of death.

Yet recent scientific advances reveal that it can take many hours for individual brain cells to die. In a 2019 *Nature* report, slaughtered pigs' brains, given a substitute blood infusion four hours after death, had brain function gradually restored over a six-to-ten-hour period. Moreover, for many years now, brain cells from human cadaver biopsies have been used to grow brain cells up to twenty hours after death, explained Parnia. His underappreciated conclusion: "Brain cells die very, very slowly," especially for those whose brains have been chilled, either medically or by drowning in cold water.

But what is death? A *Newsweek* cover showing a resuscitated heart attack victim proclaimed, "This man was dead. He isn't anymore." Parnia thinks *Newsweek* got it right. The man didn't have a "near-death experience" (NDE). He had a death experience (DE).

Ah, but *Merriam-Webster's* defines death as "a permanent cessation of all vital functions." So, I asked Parnia, has a resuscitated person actually died? Yes, he replied. Imagine two sisters simultaneously undergoing cardiac arrest, one while hiking in the Sahara Desert without help at hand, the other in a hospital ER, where she was resuscitated. Because the second could be resuscitated, would we assume that the first, in the same minutes following the cessation of heart and brain function, was not dead?

Of the 2.8 million CDC-reported deaths in the United States in 2017, Parnia cites estimates of possibly 1.1 million attempted cardiac resuscitations. So, how many of those actually get resuscitated and survive? Of these resuscitations, how many people have some memory of their death experiences (of cognitive activity during their cardiac arrest)?

For answers, Parnia offers his multisite study of 2,060

people who suffered cardiac arrests. In that group, 1,730 (84 percent) died and 330 survived. Among the survivors, 60 percent later reported no recall of their death experience. The remaining 40 percent had some recollection, including 10 percent who had a meaningful "transformative" recall. If these estimates are roughly accurate, then some eighteen thousand Americans a year recall a death experience.

NDEs (or DEs) are reportedly recalled as a peaceful and pleasant sense of being pulled toward a light, often accompanied by an out-of-body experience with a time-compressed life review. After returning to life, patients report a diminished fear of death, a kinder spirit, and more benevolent values—a "transformational" experience that Parnia hopes to study with the support of major university hospitals. In this planned study, cardiac-arrest survivors who do and don't recall cognitive experiences will complete positive psychology measures of human flourishing.

One wonders (and Parnia does, too), when did the recalled death experiences occur? During the cardiac-arrest period of brain inactivity? During the moments before and at cardiac arrest? When the resuscitated patient was gradually reemerging from a coma? Or even as a later constructed false memory?

Answers may come from a future Parnia study, focusing on aortic-repair patients, some of whom experience a controlled condition that biologically approximates death, with no heartbeat and flatlined brain activity. This version of aortic-repair surgery puts a person under anesthesia, cools the body to seventy degrees, stops the heart, and drains the blood, creating a death-like state, during which the cardiac surgeon has forty minutes to repair the aorta before warming the body and restarting the heart. Functionally, for those forty or so minutes, the patient is dead . . . but then lives again. So, will some of these people whose brains have stopped functioning experience DEs? One study suggests that at least a few aortic-repair patients, despite also being under anesthesia, do report a cognitive experience during their cardiac arrest.

Parnia hopes to take this research a step further, by exposing these "deep hypothermia" patients to stimuli during their clinical death. Afterward he will ascertain whether any of them can accurately report on events occurring while they lacked a functioning brain. (Such has been claimed by people having transformative DEs.)

Given that a positive result would be truly mind-blowing—it would challenge our understanding of the embodied person and the mind-brain connection—my colleagues and I encouraged Parnia to preregister his hypotheses and methods with the Open Science Framework (making such transparent to all), to conduct the experiment as an "adversarial collaboration" with a neuroscientist who would expect a null result, and to have credible, independent researchers gather the data, as happens with clinical safety trials.

If this experiment happens, what do you predict? Will there be someone, anyone, who will accurately report on events occurring while their brain is dormant?

Sam Parnia thinks yes. I think not.

Parnia is persuaded by his accumulation of credible-seeming accounts of resuscitated patients recalling actual happenings during their brain-inactive time. He cites the case of one young Britisher who, after all efforts to restart his heart had failed and his body turned blue, was declared dead. When the attending physician later returned to the room, he noticed that the patient's normal color was returning and discovered that his heart had somehow restarted. The next week, reported Parnia, the patient astoundingly recounted events from his death period. As Agatha Christie's Miss Marple reflected, "It wasn't what I expected. But facts are facts, and if one is proved to be wrong, one must just be humble about it and start again."

My skepticism arises from three lines of research:

1. The failure of parapsychology experiments to confirm out-of-body travel with remote viewing. (When put to the test, a would-be psychic cannot "see" happenings elsewhere, such as a card drawn by someone in an adjacent room.)

2. The mountain of cognitive neuroscience evidence linking brain and mind. (The accumulating mountain of evidence on the biology of mind suggests that every mental event is simultaneously a biological event.)

3. Scientific observations showing that brain oxygen deprivation and hallucinogenic drugs can cause similar mystical experiences (complete with the tunnel, beam of light, and life review). (Neural "funny business"—

even seizures and migraines—can produce hallucinations, including geometric patterns akin to those experienced by an oxygen-deprived brain near death.)

Nevertheless, Parnia and I agree with Miss Marple: sometimes reality surprises us.

16

DO PEOPLE REPRESS—OR VIVIDLY REMEMBER—TRAUMATIC EVENTS?

I magine yourself on a flight from Toronto to Lisbon. Five hours after takeoff and with open seas beneath you, the pilots become aware that a fractured fuel line is leaking a gallon of fuel per second. Declaring an emergency, the pilots divert toward an air base in the Azores. But still 135 miles out, one engine dies of fuel starvation, and then, some 75 miles out, the other. Moreover, your aircraft has lost its main hydraulic power, which operates the flaps.

In eerie silence, and with nothing but water beneath, you are instructed to put on a life jacket and, when hearing the countdown to ocean impact, to assume a brace position. Periodically, the pilot announces "X minutes to impact." With the ocean's surface approaching, you keep thinking, "I'm going to die."

But good news: when the engines went silent, you were

still thirty-three thousand feet in the air, and your captain is an experienced glider pilot. But bad news: you are losing some two thousand feet per minute. After minutes of descent, the pilot declares above the passengers' screams and prayers, "About to go into the water."

Then, "We have a runway! We have a runway! . . . Brace! Brace! Brace!"

Nineteen minutes after losing all engine and primary electrical power, and after a series of violent turns, the plane reaches the air base and makes a hard landing. You and 305 other passengers and crew members have escaped death. The pilots return home as heroes. And your flight becomes the subject of television dramas.

For the psychologist Margaret McKinnon, this traumatic flight was not imaginary. It was the real August 24, 2001, Air Transat Flight 236, and she, as a honeymoon passenger, was among those thinking, "I'm going to die."

Seizing this opportunity to test people's memory for details of a recorded traumatic event, McKinnon and her colleagues tracked down fifteen of her fellow passengers four years later. Seven met criteria for PTSD, such as haunting memories, jumpy anxiety, and insomnia. All of them exhibited vivid, "robust" memories of the details of their experiences.

In a follow-up study, eight of the passengers underwent fMRI brain scans while viewing a video that cued their recall of the trauma. The scans revealed "enhanced" activation in the brain's emotion processing networks, including the amygdala, two lima-bean-sized neural centers deep in the brain. This brain response (which did not appear in others who had not been on the flight) suggested that the amygdala may, via its links to the memory-forming hippocampus and visual cortical areas, help create enduring emotional memories.

The persistent memories from Flight AT236 confirm what other researchers have found—that it's much easier to forget neutral events, such as yesterday's parking place, than emotional experiences, especially extreme emotional experiences. After observing a loved one's murder, being terrorized by a hijacker or rapist, or losing one's home in a natural disaster, one may wish to forget. But such traumas are typically etched on the mind as persistent, haunting memories—for survivors of Nazi death camps, as "horror sear[ed] memory." Indeed, one of the hallmarks of PTSD is haunting, intrusive flashback memories.

So, with many forms of trauma comes not repression but, more often, robust memory. "Stronger emotional experiences make for stronger, more reliable memories," noted the memory researcher James McGaugh.

But emotional experiences also entail some noteworthy forgetting. Such was the apparent experience of the psychology professor Christine Blasey Ford, who in 2018 recalled being sexually assaulted in her teen years by the U.S. Supreme Court nominee Brett Kavanaugh, which he denied.

"She can't tell us how she got home and how she got there," scoffed Senator Lindsey Graham during a break in the Senate Judiciary hearing on Ford's testimony. For Graham, and for many other skeptics of her testimony, Ford's inability to remember simple peripheral details of that evening discounted her story's authenticity.

Studies show that stress hormones provoke the brain's amygdala to initiate, for future reference, a memory trace of the specific traumatic event: "Brain, encode this!" And to a memory scientist, a mark of stress-related memories is just such a focus on a traumatic event (in this case, a sexual assault) and what immediately preceded it—with the marginal details falling into oblivion.

To recall the event and the immediately preceding events—such as going up the stairway and into the bedroom, in Ford's case—is adaptive. It helps alert a person to future dangers. And it's also adaptive to focus, with tunnel-visioned memory, on high-priority information, with little recall of irrelevant details. Thus, whatever rivets our attention gets well recalled, at the expense of the surrounding context.

Such has been my experience during four past crises that took a family member or me to the emergency room. In each case, I vividly recall the incident (such as a broken bone). Yet in all but the most recent case, I cannot recall the trip to the hospital, the emergency room setting, or the doctors and nurses.

In our everyday life as well, our forgetting of details has a silver lining. As Williams James wrote in *The Principles of Psychology*, "If we remembered everything, we should on most occasions be as ill off as if we remembered nothing." To discard the clutter of useless or out-of-date information—where we parked the car yesterday or what our old phone number was—is surely a blessing.

17

WHEN FEAR OF LOSING STEALS OUR CHANCES OF WINNING

Would you trade lives with your nearest neighbor? Would you trade partners? Jobs? Faces?

Most people prefer the life and the things they already have. Behavioral economists and psychologists call this curious attachment to what we have the *endowment effect*. In experiments, people typically demand more to give something up than they were willing to pay to acquire it. Cornell University students given a coffee mug later demanded three times more money to sell it than other students were willing to pay for it. Buy that new lounge chair on a money-back trial and the odds are you will keep it. Ownership elicits inertia. Small wonder our homes are cluttered with things we wouldn't buy today, yet refuse to part with.

The endowment effect's corollary is *loss aversion*: we're not only attached to what we have; we hate to suffer its loss. Investors feel attached to the stocks they own and will throw good money after bad hoping to wipe out losses. After investing time and resources in a venture, business owners—having "too much invested to quit"—hesitate to abandon failing projects, even if they'd never make a new investment in a similarly troubled project. The Ford Motor Company invested $250 million in producing the ill-fated Edsel in the late 1950s. Not wanting to lock in that sunk cost, it then continued production for two and a half more years at an additional $200 million loss.

On a bigger scale, the United States sustained the Vietnam War well beyond the point where, given the circumstances, it would not have begun it. With so much invested, said Henry Kissinger, "we could not simply walk away from an enterprise involving two administrations, five allied countries, and 31,000 dead as if we were switching off a television channel."

Let's make this personal. Imagine that you are about to buy a $5,000 used car. To pay for it, you'll need to sell some of your stocks. Which of the following would you rather sell?

- $5,000 of Stock X shares, which you originally purchased for $2,500.
- $5,000 of Stock Y shares, which you originally purchased for $10,000.

Most people would rather sell Stock X and reap their $2,500 profit. One analysis of ten thousand investor accounts revealed that most people strongly prefer to lock in a profit rather than absorb a loss. Investors' *loss aversion* is curious: what matters is each stock's future value, not whether it has made or lost money in the past. (If anything, tax considerations favor selling the loser for a tax loss and avoiding the capital gains tax on the winner.)

Loss aversion is ubiquitous. Participants in experiments, where rewards are small, will choose a sure gain over flipping a coin for double or nothing. But they will readily flip a coin on a double-or-nothing chance to avert a loss. As Daniel Kahneman and Amos Tversky reported, we feel the pain from a loss twice as keenly as we feel the pleasure from a similar-sized gain. Losing $20 feels worse than finding $20 feels good. No surprise, then, that we so vigorously avoid losing in so many situations.

Loss aversion is but one example of a larger bad-is-stronger-than-good phenomenon, note Roy Baumeister and his colleagues. Bad events evoke more misery than good events evoke joy. Cruel words hurt us more than compliments please us. A bad reputation is easier to acquire—with a single lie or heartless act—than is a good reputation. "In everyday life, bad events have stronger and more lasting consequences than comparable good events." Psychologically, loss is larger than gain. Emotionally, bad is stronger than good.

Coaches and players are aware of the pain of losses, so it's no surprise that loss aversion plays out in sports. Imagine your college basketball team is behind by two points, with time only for one last shot. Would you prefer a two-point or a three-point attempt? Most coaches, wanting to avoid a loss, will seek to put the game into overtime with a two-point shot. After all, given the average 33 percent chance of making a three-point shot, such will produce a win only one-third of the time. But if the team averages 50 percent of its two-point attempts, and has about a 50 percent chance of overtime in this toss-up game, the loss-aversion strategy will yield but a 25 percent chance of sending the game to overtime, followed by an overtime victory. Thus, by averting an immediate loss, these coaches reduce the chance of an ultimate win.

Similar loss aversion affects baseball and softball base running. The statistician Peter Macdonald, the mathematician Dan McQuillan, and the computer scientist Ian McQuillan invite us to imagine "a tie game in the bottom of the ninth inning, and there is one out—a single run will win the game. You are on first base, hoping the next batter gets a hit."

As the batter hits a fly to shallow right, you hesitate between first and second to see if the sprinting outfielder will make the catch. When the outfielder traps rather than catches the ball, you zoom to second. The next batter hits a fly to center field and, alas, the last batter strikes out.

You probably didn't question this cautious base-running scenario, because it's what players do and what coaches commend. But consider an alternative strategy, say Macdonald and his colleagues. If you had risked running to third on that first fly ball, you would have scored the winning run on the ensuing fly ball. Using data from thirty-two years of Major League Baseball, the researchers calculate that anytime a fly ball is at least 38 percent likely to fall for a hit, the runner should abandon caution and streak for third. Yet, when there's a 38 percent (or a bit more) chance of a hit, that running strategy "is never attempted."

You may object that players cannot compute probabilities. But, says the Macdonald team, "players and their third-base coaches make these sorts of calculations all the time. They gamble on sacrifice flies and stolen base attempts using probabilities of success." Nevertheless, when it comes to running from first, their main goal is to avert loss—and to avoid, even at the cost of a possible run, the risk of looking like a fool. We implicitly think, "What if I fail?" before "How can I succeed?"

Often in life, it seems, our excessive fear of losing subverts our opportunities to win. Caution thwarts triumph. In sports as in life, little ventured, little gained.

18

HOW WE POLARIZE, AND WHAT WE CAN DO ABOUT IT

Red and blue partisans alike are aghast at what others believe and support. As one incredulous friend recently said of his family, "I can't believe that I personally know people who are so foolish." This divided family is not alone. Would you be unhappy if your child married someone from the other party? From 1960 to 2019, the percent of folks answering yes shot up from 4 to 40 percent.

U.S. legislators have likewise polarized. In 1965, thirteen Republican senators joined with their Democratic counterparts to approve public Medicare. In 2010, no Republican joined with Democrats to approve Obamacare. Ditto the American Rescue Plan Act of 2021.

What psychological forces are driving and sustaining our great and growing divide? As I will later explain, *belief perseverance* solidifies ideas when our explanations of why they might be true outlast the discrediting of evidence that inspired them. *Motivated reasoning* justifies what we already believe or want to believe. And *confirmation bias* motivates our search for belief-confirming evidence.

There is also a powerful fourth phenomenon: *group polarization*, which further amplifies the shared views of like-minded folks. When like minds discuss, their attitudes often become more extreme. Like hot coals, like minds strengthen one another.

Long ago, George Bishop and I invited high-prejudice students (based on their earlier answers to an attitude inventory) to discuss racial issues with others (who, unknown to them, were of like mind). We did the same with low-prejudice students. As we reported in *Science*, the result was group polarization: the divide between the two groups grew. Separation + conversation → polarization.

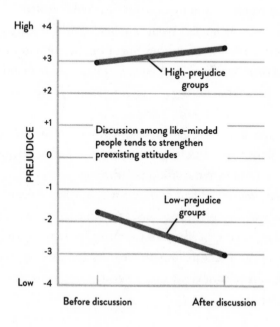

Group polarization also occurs in courtrooms. When jury members lean toward awarding damages, their group award tends to exceed that preferred by the median jury member. Likewise, observed David Schkade and Cass Sunstein, "a Republican appointee sitting with two other Republicans votes far more conservatively than when the same judge sits with at least one Democratic appointee. A Democratic appointee, meanwhile, shows the same tendency in the opposite ideological direction." Opinion diversity moderates views; like minds polarize.

The phenomenon can work for good, as when peacemakers, hunger advocates, and Black Lives Matter activists gain strength from connecting with kindred spirits. Or it can be toxic, as when like minds amplify bigotry, intensify conspiracy paranoia, and overwhelm our skeptic system.

Terrorist mentality usually emerges slowly, among people who share a grievance. As they interact in isolation (sometimes with other "brothers" and "sisters" in camps or in prisons), their views grow more extreme. Increasingly, they categorize the world as "us" against "them."

People have long gained conviction from the meeting of like minds. But three more recent cultural changes provide fertile soil for extreme group polarization.

The internet: When cutting my scientific eyeteeth doing group polarization experiments, I never imagined the benefits, and the dangers, of like-minded virtual groups. Today's progressives can friend fellow progressives and link one another to sites that affirm views they share and disparage views they despise. Conservatives do likewise. The end result? Partisanship veers toward tribalism.

Partisan cable TV: But the internet is far from the whole story, because polarization has deepened even among those least likely to use it. The soil that nourishes polarization also includes today's politicized cable television options. In the past, a handful of mainstream news sources fed us all. Today, we can choose like-minded news—think Fox and MSNBC evening talk shows—that reinforce our existing views.

The geography of division: There is also a third and less obvious social phenomenon at work. In a contest between proverbs—do "opposites attract," or do "birds of a feather flock together"?—one of social psychology's oldest and most firmly established principles is that *similarity attracts.*

Opposites attracting can make for a good story: Think Frog and Toad. Or: "I'm Aquarius—decisive. He's Libra—indecisive. We complement each other with so little conflict, because he's happy when I make the arrangements."

But in reality, people are drawn to those with whom they share attitudes, beliefs, interests, age, religion, education, intelligence, economic status . . . the list goes on. We could wish it were otherwise, because there are benefits to diversity in neighborhoods and work teams. Yet birds who flock together—rich birds, tall birds, pretty birds, smoker birds, evangelical birds—typically are of a feather. Likeness leads to liking. Similarity breeds content.

And that helps explain why, in an age of increased mobility (we more often live at some distance from our original home), our internet/TV social bubbles are compounded by geographic bubbles, where people live among other like-minded folks. Blue counties have become a deeper blue, and red counties a brighter red. As Philip Bump reports, the Democratic presidential candidate's margin in Democratic-voting counties increased from an average 15 percent in 2000 to 23 percent in 2020, while the average Republican candidate's margin in Republican-voting counties increased from 26 to 43 percent. Whether you live in rural Wyoming or in central Seattle, just about everyone you meet likely thinks the way you do.

This increasing geographic segregation of like minds helps explain the astounding result of a September 2020 Pew survey: four in ten Biden and Trump supporters said they did "not have a single close friend" who supported the other candidate. As I am, so are my friends.

Our world faces mammoth challenges: preventing a climate apocalypse, reducing systemic racism and hyper-inequality, and building bridges of understanding across our partisan chasm. For better and for worse, the internet, cable television, and geographic mobility will endure. So how might we depolarize?

Technologists can surely help, by prioritizing Mark Zuckerberg's original vision of "a more connected world." By flagging demonstrable untruths, creating forums for "deliberative democracy," and linking people across boundaries, future technologies can work at increasing shared understandings.

Citizen initiatives can engage dialogue. Nonprofit organizations working to depolarize America include Living Room Conversations, the Civil Conversations Project, the Depolarization Project, and Braver Angels, which is bringing red and blue together "to understand the other side's point of view . . . to look for common ground . . . and to support principles that bring us together rather than divide us." For some specific policies, such as higher taxes on the superrich, net neutrality, and a $15 minimum wage, there is already bipartisan supermajority support.

Educators can advance understanding. Education aims to counter the power of misinformation and "anecdata" by teaching evidence-based critical thinking. Education can also work at enabling people, even when disagreeing, to understand others' perspectives. It can train intellectual humility ("What's the weakest part of my argument? What's the strongest part of my opponent's argument?"). And, with our attention so often drawn to how we differ, educators can teach listening skills that enable us to appreciate our shared concerns and values. One example is the evidence-based, ready-to-use online pedagogy offered by openmindplatform.org.

The utopian goal is not a *Nineteen Eighty-Four*–like uniformity of public opinion. Rather, our challenge is to affirm both our diversity *and* our unifying ideals, and so to renew the founding idea of America: diversity within unity. *E pluribus unum*: out of many, one.

19

OUR DIFFERENCES SEIZE OUR ATTENTION, DEFINE OUR IDENTITY, AND SOMETIMES DECEIVE US

S elf-consciousness," noted C. S. Lewis in *The Problem of Pain*, exists "in contrast with an 'other,' a something which is not the self." We are, always and everywhere, self-conscious of how we differ. Search your memory for a social situation in which you were the only person of your gender, sexual orientation, ethnicity, or body type. Perhaps you were the only woman in a group of men, or the only straight person at an LGBTQ gathering.

Recalling that situation . . .

- Were you self-conscious about your identity?
- How did others respond to you?
- How did your perceptions of their responses affect your behavior?

Differences determine our "spontaneous self-concepts." If you recalled being very aware of your differences, you are not alone. As the social psychologist William McGuire long ago noted, we are conscious of ourselves "insofar as, and in the ways that," we differ. When he and his co-workers invited children to "tell us about yourself," they mostly mentioned their distinctive attributes. Redheads volunteered their hair color, foreign-born their birthplace, minority children their ethnicity. In the United States, a Pew survey finds that 74 percent of Black people but only 15 percent of white people see their race as "being extremely or very important to how they think of themselves."

Spontaneous self-concepts often adapt to a changing group. A Black woman among white women will think of herself as Black, McGuire observed. When moving to a group of Black men, she will become more conscious of being a woman. In *Caste: The Origins of Our Discontents*, Isabel Wilkerson quotes a Nigerian-born playwright: "You know that there are no black people in Africa . . . They are Igbo and Yoruba, Ewe, Akan, Ndebele. They are not black . . . They don't become black until they go to America or come to the U.K."

Even when the people of two cultures are nearly identical, they will still notice their differences. Small distinctions may provoke scorn. Jonathan Swift satirized the phenomenon in his book *Gulliver's Travels* in describing the war between the Big-Endians and their neighbors. Their difference: only the Big-Endians preferred to break their eggs on the large end.

This identity-shaping phenomenon affects us all. When serving on an American Psychological Association professional task force with ten others—all women—I immediately was aware of my gender. But it was only on the second day, when I joked to the woman next to me that the bathroom break line would be short for me, that she noticed the group's gender makeup. In my daily life, surrounded by mostly white colleagues and neighbors, I am seldom cognizant of my race, which becomes a prominent part of my identity when visiting my daughter in South Africa, where I become part of a 9 percent minority. In Scotland, I'm self-conscious of being American. To be in a numerical minority is to become more conscious of that identity.

Our differences may influence how others respond to us. Researchers have also noted a related phenomenon: our differences, though mostly salient to ourselves, may also affect how others treat us. Being the "different" or "solo" person—a Black person in an otherwise white group, a woman in a male group, or an adult in a group of children—can make a person more visible and seem more influential. Their good and bad qualities also tend to be more noticed.

If we differ from others around us, it therefore makes adaptive sense for us to be a bit wary. It makes sense for a salient person—a minority race person, a gay person, or a corpulent person—to be alert and sensitive to how they are being treated by an interviewer, a police officer, or a neighbor. Explicit prejudices and implicit biases are real, and stereotypes of a difference can become a self-fulfilling prophecy.

Sometimes our perceived differences influence not only how others treat us but also how we, in turn, respond to them. Recall from chapter 11 the experiment in which men conversed by phone with women they mistakenly presumed (from having been shown a fake picture) were either conventionally unattractive or attractive. The presumed attractive women were later rated as speaking more warmly. The men's beliefs had led them to act in a way that influenced the women to fulfill the belief that beautiful women are desirable. The beauty stereotype had become a self-fulfilling prophecy.

Imagine yourself as one of the sixty young men or sixty young women in a follow-up experiment by Robert Ridge and Jeffrey Reber. Each man interviewed one of the women. Before doing so, he was told that she felt either attracted to him (based on his responses to a biographical questionnaire) or not attracted. The result, again, was behavioral confirmation: women believed to be feeling an attraction actually exhibited more flirtatiousness (in response to the man's behavior). This process writ large, Ridge and Reber speculated, sometimes contributes to sexual harassment. If a man's beliefs evoke a confirming response, he may then misinterpret her warmth and inappropriately escalate his overtures.

Our acute self-consciousness of our differences can cause us to exaggerate or misinterpret others' reactions. At times, our acute self-consciousness of our differences may have funny consequences. In one of social psychology's more creative studies, Robert Kleck and Angelo Strenta used theatrical makeup to place an ear-to-mouth facial scar on college women—supposedly to see how others would react. After each woman checked the real-looking scar in a hand mirror, the experimenter applied "moisturizer" to "keep the makeup from cracking"—but which actually removed the scar.

So the scene was set: A woman, feeling terribly self-conscious about her supposedly scarred face, talks with another woman who knows nothing of all this. If you have ever felt similarly self-conscious—perhaps about a physical handicap, acne, even just a bad hair day—then perhaps you can sympathize with the woman. Compared with women who were led to believe their conversational partners merely thought they had an allergy, the "disfigured" women became acutely sensitive to how their partners were looking at them. They rated their partners as more tense, distant, and patronizing. Observers who later analyzed videotapes of how the partners treated "disfigured" persons could find no such differences in treatment. Self-conscious about being different, the "disfigured" women had misinterpreted normal mannerisms and comments.

Our self-consciousness of how we differ can similarly distort the everyday experiences of well-intentioned people. Imagine that Bob, an out gay man, meets straight Ben, who is accepting and wanting to respond without prejudice. But feeling unsure of himself and not wanting to risk saying anything offensive, Ben holds back a bit. Bob, who has learned to expect negative attitudes from most people in his town, misreads Ben's hesitancy as hostility and responds accordingly.

Consider, also, one of social psychology's most provocative yet simplest experiments. Cornell University students were asked to don a Barry Manilow T-shirt (at the behest of the researcher Thomas Gilovich and colleagues) and were then shown into a room where several others were completing questionnaires. Afterward they were asked to guess how many of the others noticed their dorky attire. Their estimate? About half. Actually, only 23 percent did.

This *spotlight effect*—an overestimation of others' noticing us, as if a spotlight were shining on us—extends to our secret emotions. Thanks to an *illusion of transparency*, we presume that our attractions, our disgust, and our anxieties leak out and become visible to others. Imagine standing before an audience: If we're nervous and we know it, will our face surely show it? Not necessarily. Even our lies and our lusts are less transparent than we imagine.

There's bad news here: others notice us less than we imagine (partly because they are more worried about the impressions *they* are making).

But there's also good news: others notice us less than we imagine. And that good news is liberating: A bad hair day hardly matters. And if we wear yesterday's clothes again today, few will notice. Fewer will care. Of those, fewer still will remember.

20

THE PSYCHOLOGY OF DIVISION

t has boggled our minds: Sunni and Shia—both revering the Quran, following Muhammad, and praying to Allah—killing one another. It brings to mind the more than thirty-five hundred dead from the clashes between Northern Ireland's Protestants and Catholics—all, at least nominally, following the same Prince of Peace.

Why such animosity among those so ethnically and religiously similar? Sunni-Shia violence and Protestant-Catholic clashes both have deep historical-political roots. As the late Ed Cairns, leader of the University of Ulster's Peace and Conflict Research Group, once told me, religious labels often represent cultural rather than religious identities: "If anything, the more [Northern Irelanders actually] believed or went to church, the less prejudice they showed."

Group polarization helps explain why small differences often loom so large. As we've seen, groups polarize as like-minded folks connect and discuss. Within the echo chambers of like-minded networks, viewpoints become more extreme. White supremacists become more racist. Anti-vaxxers become more immune to evidence. For good or ill, socially networked birds of a feather gain support for their shared beliefs and inclinations. Suspicion becomes conviction. Disagreements escalate to demonization.

Three additional group psychology principles further explain the intensity of clashes among kindred folk.

1. No matter our similarities with others, our attention focuses on differences. Recall from the previous chapter, when William McGuire invited children to "tell us about yourself," they zeroed in on their distinctive hair color, race, or foreign birth. Ditto with adults: straight folks sometimes wonder why gay folks are so conscious of their sexual identity, though in a predominantly gay culture the sexual identity self-consciousness would be reversed. Speaking at LGBT gatherings, I have been self-conscious of my heterosexuality.

Even when people of two subcultures are nearly identical, they often overlook their kinship and become laser focused on their small differences. Freud recognized this phenomenon: "Of two neighboring towns, each is the other's most jealous rival; every little canton looks down upon the others with contempt. Closely related races keep one another at arm's length; the South German cannot endure the North German, the Englishman casts every kind of aspersion upon the Scot, the Spaniard despises the Portuguese."

2. We naturally divide our worlds into "us" and "them," in-group and out-group. We inherited our Stone Age ancestors' need to belong, to live in groups. There was safety in solidarity. Whether hunting, defending, or attacking, ten hands were better than two. Like them, we form social identities. We define who is in our group and who is other. Even our co-workers or classmates we may divide into those inside and those outside the group we identify with. Moreover, having a *social identity*—a sense of "we-ness"—bolsters our self-concept. It feels good to take pride in one's group.

But the benefits come at a cost. Mentally drawing a circle that defines "us" also defines "them." Moreover, an "in-group bias"—a preference for one's own community—soon follows. In experiments, even those in arbitrarily created groups tend to favor their own group. In studies by Henri Tajfel, Michael Billig, and others, people grouped together by something as random as a coin toss or the last digit of their driver's licenses felt a twinge of kinship with their number mates and favored their own group when dividing rewards.

3. Group solidarity soars when facing a common enemy. From laboratory experiments to America immediately after the September 11 attacks, shared threats foster unity. During conflict, we-feeling rises. During wars, patriotism surges.

In one of psychology's more famous and now controversial experiments, the psychologist Muzafer Sherif randomly split Oklahoma City boy campers into two groups for a series of competitive activities, with prizes for the victors. Over the ensuing two weeks, in-group pride and out-group hostility increased—marked by food wars, fistfights, and ransacked cabins. Intergroup contacts yielded more threats—and stronger feelings of in-group unity—until Sherif engaged the boys in cooperative efforts toward shared goals, such as moving a stuck truck or restoring the camp's water supply.

In more playful ways, these group dynamics also fuel

sports rivalries. Think Yankees–Red Sox, March Madness, and World Cup soccer. For an ardent Cubs fan, it's a good day if the Cubs win—or the White Sox lose.

Here in western Michigan, America's biggest small-college sports rivalry plays out whenever my school, Hope College, plays Calvin University, pitting the Dutch-heritage Reformed Church in America tradition against the Dutch-heritage Christian Reformed Church tradition—extending the two churches' 1857 split over what now seem like minor matters. It's all in good fun, an intense competition with no fundamental hate. But when the social dynamics are writ large, people will not only cheer for their groups; they may also kill and die for them.

Turning today's closed fists into tomorrow's open arms requires recognizing the relative modesty of our overblown differences, finding our deeper commonalities, defining a larger "us," communicating across group lines, and discovering transcendent goals.

Such conflict resolution is most needed, yet most difficult, in times of crisis. When conflicts intensify, images become more stereotyped, judgments more rigid, communication more difficult. Both sides are prone to threaten, coerce, or retaliate. The challenge is for cultures to discover what the social psychologist Fathali Moghaddam calls an "omnicultural" perspective that both recognizes commonalities and respects differences. From Iraq to Northern Ireland, the Koreas to the Sudans, this is the great challenge in times of conflict—to embrace "diversity within unity."

21

THE SOCIAL PSYCHOLOGY OF DISSENT

n a 1951 experiment by the Columbia University social psychologist Stanley Schachter, groups discussed how to deal with the fictional juvenile delinquent "Johnny Rocco." One "modal" group member (actually Schachter's accomplice) concurred with the others in arguing for leniency and became well liked. A second accomplice, the "deviate," stood alone in arguing for harsh discipline. At first, the study participants argued with the nonconforming deviate, but eventually they ignored him and then reported disliking him.

Recent experiments with both children and adults confirm the lesson: groups respond harshly to members who deviate from group norms and threaten their group identity. Other studies show how agonizingly difficult it can be to publicly state truths after hearing consensus falsehoods from one's peers and how "groupthink" suppresses dissent. After President John F. Kennedy's ill-fated Bay of Pigs invasion, his adviser Arthur Schlesinger Jr., having self-censored his misgivings, reproached himself "for having kept so silent during those crucial discussions."

To dissent from one's group—one's fraternity, one's religion, one's friends—can be painful, especially when a minority of one.

Mitt Romney understands. For being a minority of one Republican in voting for President Trump's removal, he anticipated being "vehemently denounced. I'm sure to hear abuse from the President and his supporters."

And he was denounced. "I don't like people who use their faith as justification for doing what they know is wrong," vented the president, before ridiculing Romney for "one of the worst campaigns in the history of the presidency." Donald Trump Jr. went further, calling for Romney to "be expelled" from the GOP. Romney, some congressional colleagues derided, was a "sore loser" who acted "to appease the left" and was "not very collegial."

The rewards of conformity, and the rejection of dissenters, are no secret. As President Kennedy recalled in *Profiles in Courage* (1955), "'The way to get along,' I was told when I entered Congress, 'is to go along.'" It is a temptation we all face. When feeling alone, we may silence our voice. We may join a standing ovation for something we do not inwardly applaud. We may succumb to the power of our herd and its leader.

And then, feeling some dissonance over conforming, we rationalize. Observing our own silence and our false witness, our mind mutates, and we begin to believe what we reluctantly stood up for. Our attitudes follow our actions, which grow their own self-justifying legs. As C. S. Lewis noted in

Mere Christianity, "Every time you make a choice you are turning the central part of you, the part of you that chooses, into something a little different from what it was before."

For those who endure the distress of dissent, there are benefits.

1. *Minorities of one can matter.* "All history," wrote Ralph Waldo Emerson, "is a record of the power of minorities, and of minorities of one." Think of Copernicus and Galileo, or of Rosa Parks's refusal to sit at the back of the bus. In the short term, these heroes, and the conformity-resisting former senators whom Kennedy later celebrated in *Profiles in Courage*, were scorned for flouting team play and resisting expectations. It was only later that historians and filmmakers honored their heroism. Mitt Romney can take the long view.

2. *Experiments on "minority influence" show how a minority of one can matter.* When such individuals, despite ridicule, *persist with consistency*—without waffling—they can sway their laboratory group, or even change history. In experiments, the French social psychologist Serge Moscovici found that if a numerical minority consistently judged blue slides as green, the majority would occasionally agree, but never if the minority wavered in their judgments. Likewise, in simulated juries, a minority of two accomplices working for an experimenter sometimes stimulate the majority to rethink its position, but only if they persist.

In August 2018, the fifteen-year-old Swedish schoolgirl Greta Thunberg initiated the first school strike protesting climate change by sitting alone outside the Swedish Parliament beside her SKOLSTREJK FÖR KLIMATET (School strike for climate) sign. As she persisted, others followed. Thirteen months later, four million joined her worldwide climate strike, and *Time* honored her as 2019 Person of the Year. This is the power of one.

Being a persistent dissenting voice may get you disliked. The pain of being a dissenting minority explains a "minority slowness effect"—a tendency for those with minority views to speak up more reluctantly than do people in the majority. Still, persistence may stimulate others' rethinking. When the social psychologist Charlan Nemeth placed a two-person minority within simulated juries and instructed them to contest the majority's view, the duo was routinely disliked. Yet the majority members acknowledged that the two provoked them to rethink their positions. Other experiments find that opinion minorities can stimulate deeper thinking that leads to creative innovation.

Dissent punctures the illusion of unanimity, which can also enable others to express their doubts. Dissent is especially potent when it is expressed with forceful *self-confidence* and when it represents a *defection* from the majority. It's harder for Republicans to dismiss the Republican Mitt Romney than it is for Republicans to dismiss the Democrat Alexandria Ocasio-Cortez. He's one of their own; she is not. As in the film classic *12 Angry Men*, in which one lone juror eventually wins over eleven other jurors, defections from the majority can seed more defections, sometimes in a snowball effect.

Transformational leaders often exhibit the consistency, persistence, and self-confidence that help make a minority view persuasive. They welcome diverse views. But their consistency and charisma, and their ability to communicate a vision in clear and simple language, also win their followers' trust and allegiance.

If single individuals plant themselves indomitably on their instincts, "and there abide," wrote Emerson, "the huge world will come round."

22

THE OVERCONFIDENCE
PHENOMENON

The greatest enemy of knowledge is not ignorance—it is the illusion of knowledge."

This wisdom, often attributed to the American historian Daniel Boorstin, suggests a sister aphorism: *The great enemy of democracy is not ill will, but the illusion of understanding.* Democracy is undermined by social and political opinion that, even if sincerely believed, sprouts from misinformed self-confidence.

That modern reality illustrates one of psychology's most reliable phenomena: the *overconfidence phenomenon*—the tendency, when making judgments and forecasts, to be more confident than correct. We routinely think we know more than we do. Asked how sure we are of our answers to factual questions (Is Boston north or south of Paris?), we tend to be more confident than correct.* And when 60 percent of people correctly

---

* Boston is south of Paris.

answer a factual question, such as "Is absinthe a liqueur or a precious stone?" they will typically feel 75 percent confident.

Overconfident stockbrokers market their advice regarding which stocks will likely rise while other stockbrokers give opposite advice (with a stock's current price being the balance point between them). But in the long run, essentially *none* of them will beat the market.

The social psychologist Philip Tetlock collected more than twenty-seven thousand expert predictions of world events, such as the future of South Africa or whether Quebec would separate from Canada. His repeated finding: the predictions, made with 80 percent confidence on average, were 40 percent right. Nevertheless, even those who erred maintained their confidence by noting they were "almost right": "The Québécois separatists almost won the secessionist referendum."

Paul Krugman has described similar overconfidence and reluctance to admit error among economists and politicians:

- When Bill Clinton raised taxes on the rich, some politicians and economists predicted economic disaster, but the economy instead boomed, with twenty-three million jobs added during the Clinton years.
- When Kansas politicians passed large tax cuts with the promise that growth would pay for them, the result was an unexpected state funding crisis.
- When, in 2008, the Federal Reserve responded to the recession by cutting interest rates to zero, conservative economists and pundits published an open letter warning of soaring inflation to come. But it didn't.

When none of the predicted economic outcomes happened, did the forecasters own their error and change their thinking? Contacted by Bloomberg, not one of the inflation open letter signatories acknowledged error. Instead, they offered (in Krugman's words) "some reason wrong was right . . . and never, ever, an admission that maybe something was wrong with [their] initial analysis."

Such is not the province of any one political perspective. Consider: A CivicScience poll asked 3,624 Americans if schools should "teach Arabic numerals as part of their curriculum." Fifty-six percent answered no. Among Republican respondents, 74 percent objected; among Democrats, the number was 40 percent. (Do the respondents advise, instead, teaching Roman numerals?) CivicScience also asked people if schools should teach the "creation theory of Catholic priest Georges Lemaitre as part of their science curriculum." Unlike the 33 percent of Republicans who objected, 73 percent of Democrats opposed such teaching . . . of the big bang theory.

Such illusions of understanding are powered by the overconfidence phenomenon and also by a sister phenomenon—the famed *Dunning-Kruger effect*. Those who score *lowest* on grammar, humor, and logic tests, David Dunning and Justin Kruger reported, tend to be the most likely to *over*estimate their abilities. Incompetence doesn't recognize itself. "Our ignorance is invisible to us," notes Dunning. "The first rule of the Dunning-Kruger club is you don't know you're a member of the Dunning-Kruger club."

Thus, ignorance can, ironically, feed overconfidence. Ignorant of my ignorance—and therefore prone to over-confidence—I am blissfully unaware of all the possible Scrabble words I fail to see. And that enables me to think myself verbally adept. We are, as Daniel Kahneman has said, often "blind to our [cognitive] blindness." To that I would add—mindful that us folks with hearing loss are often the last to notice (because we're unaware of what we've not heard)—that we can also be deaf to our own deafness. We don't know what we don't know.

We're even prone to overconfidence about what we should know best—ourselves. Robert Vallone and his colleagues discovered as much when they, in September, invited college students to predict whether they would drop a course, choose to live off campus the next year, and so forth. The students felt, on average, 84 percent sure of their self-predictions. But they erred nearly twice as often as they anticipated. Even when 100 percent confident, they were right only 85 percent of the time.

The resulting misinformed overconfidence matters. Some examples: When—despite plummeting violent and property crime rates—seven in ten adults annually believe there has been more crime in the current year than in the prior year, fearmongering politicians may triumph. When immigrants crossing the southern U.S. border are seen as oftentimes "vicious predators and bloodthirsty killers"—notwithstanding immigrants' somewhat lower actual crime and incarceration rates—there will be calls to "build the wall." In 2021, unvaccinated people were more blasé about COVID-19 than were vaccinated people, and a public health crisis resulted.

As the late Hans Rosling and his family amply documented in their bestselling *Factfulness*, ignorance often reigns. Even with this forewarning, consider: What percent of the world's one-year-olds have had a vaccination? What percent of humanity lives in extreme poverty (less than $2 a day)? What percent of humanity is literate (able to read and write)? The factual answers—86 percent, 9 percent, and 86 percent, respectively—differ radically from Americans' perceptions. Their vaccination estimate: 35 percent. And though extreme poverty has plummeted and literacy has soared, most don't know that. More than people suppose, the arc of history is bending in favorable directions, with substantial improvements in world health, education, and prosperity.

Overconfidence also feeds the planning fallacy. Students and construction planners often expect to finish projects on or ahead of schedule. In fact, they often generally take about twice the predicted time. College students writing a senior thesis paper finished three weeks later than their "most realistic" estimate and a week later than their "worst-case scenario" estimate. The Boston Big Dig tunnel, which was scheduled for a 1998 completion costing $2.8 billion, was completed in 2007 for more than $8 billion.

The planning fallacy colors our personal judgments as well. It leads us to be up later than we planned to finish an assignment, to arrive late at our destination, or, anticipating how much more time we will have next month or next year, to accept invitations that we later regret.

Perhaps, then, we should all aspire to a greater spirit of humility. Although we mortals are more than "headpieces filled with straw," we are finite and fallible. We have dignity but not deity. And that is why we should hold our own judgments tentatively, assess other people's actions with open-minded skepticism, and, when appropriate, use science and evidence to separate error from truth. As Confucius reminds us, "When you know a thing, to hold that you know it; and when you do not know a thing, to allow that you do not know it; this is knowledge."

23

WHY IS EVERYONE ELSE HAVING MORE FUN?

Think for a moment: Who goes to more parties—you or others?

Across eleven studies, Cornell University's Sebastian Deri and his colleagues found that university students, mall shoppers, and online respondents perceived others' social lives to be more active than their own duller life. Other folks, it seems, party more, dine out more, and have more friends and fun.

The Deri team has an explanation for why most people perceive their social lives as comparatively inactive. Our social perceptions, they note, suffer from biased information availability. We compare ourselves not with social reality but with what's mentally accessible. We hear more about our friends' activities than we do about the nonevents of their lives. We're more likely to hear about Alexis going to a party than about her sitting home staring at the TV over her toes.

Such social comparisons lie at the heart of social media.

In founding Facebook, Mark Zuckerberg, once a psychology student, envisioned social *benefits*. His declared mission: "to make the world more open and connected."

Later research suggests that Facebook partially succeeded. The social psychologists Jenna Clark, Sara Algoe, and Melanie Green explain that "research has empirically distinguished between passive Facebook use (defined as consuming information without direct exchanges) and active Facebook use (defined as activities that facilitate direct exchanges with others)." They concluded that moderate, interactive social media use supports and broadens our social connections.

It's the passive use—just reading others' feeds—that predicts lower well-being. This is thanks partly to our human propensity for *social comparison*. To decide if we are poor or rich, fat or svelte, dumb or smart, we compare ourselves with others. Students at less selective schools have better academic self-concepts than those surrounded by brilliant students. We feel smart when others seem dimwitted, rich when exposed to poverty, and athletic around the klutzy. When comparing downward, we may even experience Schadenfreude—pleasure in another's failure.

More often, we compare upward, which explains why social media amplifies our sense of social disadvantage. People post selfies while out having fun—which we may browse while sitting home alone. When others' posts make them seem happy, popular, and successful, it's natural to feel a twinge of envy. When we see them having wonderful, loving connections with their children or parents, we, mindful of our more mundane or conflicted lives, often feel a bit depressed.

As Teddy Roosevelt long ago surmised, "Comparison is the thief of joy."

So, does your life seem pallid compared with all the fun others appear to be having? Do you believe you are not one of the socially active "cool" people? Does your romantic life seem comparatively unexciting? Do you wish you could have as many friends as others seem to?

Well, be consoled: most of your friends feel the same way.

The others-are-having-more-fun finding joins other reports of social media's psychological effects. For example, what should we make of the simple fact that the spread of smartphones and social media has precisely paralleled a recent increase in teen loneliness, depression, and suicide? Consider:

1. The changes in how we humans connect and compare have been fast and vast. Worldwide, smartphones and easier social media access exploded, with most humans now having broadband mobile subscriptions. In the United States, 2010's sixty-three million smartphone users had more than quadrupled by 2020.

2. Simultaneously—and coincidentally?—American, Canadian, and British teen girls' rates of depression, anxiety, self-harm, and suicide ballooned. From 2010 to 2018, a U.S. National Survey on Drug Use and Health reveals, major depressive episodes soared from 8 to 14 percent among both twelve-to-seventeen-year-olds and eighteen-to-twenty-five-year-olds. In its follow-up monitoring of "youth risk behavior," the CDC similarly reported that the share of teens feeling

"sad or hopeless" had increased from 26 to 37 percent since 2009. Moreover, both youth and young adults experienced a corresponding sharp increase in suicidal thoughts and suicide attempts.

So, is the depression/suicidal thinking increase that accompanied the smartphone/social media increase a mere coincidence—or is there a causal connection? If so, is it big enough to matter?

To explore a possible social media/depression connection, my social psychologist colleagues Jonathan Haidt and Jean Twenge have assembled the available evidence using three psychological methods.

1. Correlational (associational) studies ask, *is actual social media use associated with teen mental health?* Study outcomes vary, but overall there is at least a small correlation between adolescents' social media hours and their risk of depression, anxiety, and self-harm. The screen time–disorder association is stronger for social media use than for TV and gaming time, and the link is greater for females who are heavy social media users. Twenge, who is now my co-author of *Social Psychology*, 14th edition, and author of *iGen*, reports that "teens who visit social-networking sites every day but see their friends in person less frequently are the most likely to agree with the statements 'A lot of times I feel lonely,' 'I often feel left out of things,' and 'I often wish I had more good friends.'"

2. Longitudinal studies (following lives through time) ask, *does today's social media use predict future mental health?* In six of eight studies, the answer is yes.

3. Experiments (controlled tests of one factor) ask, *do volunteers randomly assigned to restricted social media use fare better than those who were not on outcomes such as loneliness and depression?* On balance, yes, says Haidt, but the few such studies have produced mixed results. One recent study randomly assigned three thousand paid volunteers to either deactivate their Facebook account or not. The result: "Four weeks without Facebook improved subjective well-being."

Part of this social media time effect simply results from the internet's time-sucking social costs. When internet use first soared, face-to-face time with family and friends declined. Moreover, the internet has displaced time from everything else (speaking, sleeping, snogging).

Smartphones have especially transformed the world of teens. With increased time online, today's teens spend less time dating, driving, drinking, working, reading, and talking face-to-face. The time drain adds up to more than most folks realize. In one study, people estimated they checked their phones thirty-seven times a day. Actually, it was eighty-five times daily. Life is online. Check in or miss out.

What advice, then, do Haidt and Twenge have for parents? Should parents give (or deny) their middle schoolers smartphones with Instagram or Snapchat accounts? And does the amount of daily screen time matter?

Haidt tweeted his recommendation of three parental "norms":

1) all screens out of bedroom 30 min before bedtime;
2) no social media until high school;
3) time limits on total daily device use (such as two hours or less).

Twenge offered kindred advice for parents concerned about their children's social media use:

- "No phone or tablets in the bedroom at night."
- "No using devices within an hour of bedtime."
- "Limit device time to less than two hours of leisure time a day."

Stay tuned. This scientific story is still being written, amid some conflicting results. But as Twenge summarizes, up to two hours of daily screen time predicts no lessening of teen well-being. Indeed, online networking does "make the world more open and connected." It sustains our relationships with friends and family and offers support when we're down. But as daily screen time increases to six hours—with associated diminishing of face-to-face relationships, sleep, exercise, reading, and time outdoors—the risk of depression and anxiety rises.

The drastic rise in youth and young adult depression, especially over such a thin slice of history, demands our attention. Is screen time the major culprit (both for its drain on other healthy activities and for the upward social comparisons of one's own mundane life with the lives of cooler-seeming others)? If not, what other social forces are at work? And what can be done to protect and improve youth and young adult well-being?

24

SOCIAL FACILITATION: THE ENERGIZING PRESENCE OF OTHERS

The recent COVID-19 pandemic mandated "social distancing" for students gathering in classrooms, people gathering for worship, and fans gathering for events. Although some social psychologists suggested that "*physical* distancing" would be the more apt term, the distancing effects were genuinely social. As social psychology's most venerable research reminds us, physical closeness generates social energy.

In one of the discipline's first experiments, Norman Triplett reported in 1898 that teens wound fishing reels faster when other "co-acting" teens were nearby doing the same. "The bodily presence of another . . . serves to liberate latent energy," Triplett concluded.

Although Triplett's finding fell short of statistical significance, many ensuing experiments confirmed the energizing power of others' presence. In the company of others, people more swiftly solved simple multiplication problems and crossed out specified letters. This *social facilitation phenomenon* even occurred with animals. In the presence of others of their species, ants moved more sand. Sexually active rats mated more often. And chickens ate more grain.

But there was a problem. Some studies found the presence of others actually *hindered* performance. With others co-acting or looking on, people became *less* adept at completing a maze, solving complex multiplication problems, or learning nonsense syllables. And birds likewise learned mazes more slowly in the presence of other birds.

To say that others' presence sometimes boosts performance and sometimes undercuts it is about as helpful as a Seattle weather forecast in March predicting sun or showers. After grinding to an unsatisfying halt by 1940, social facilitation research lay dormant for a quarter century until awakened by the hand of one of the greatest knights of social psychology's roundtable.

As often happens at creative scientific moments, Robert Zajonc (rhymes with "science") reconciled these contradictory findings by shining the light of another well-known psychological science principle: *arousal enhances dominant responses*. The principle rightly predicted that arousal *improves* performance on easy tasks (for which the dominant first response is correct). For example, people solved easy anagrams, such as "akec," fastest when aroused by the presence of others. And arousal *inhibits* performance on hard tasks (for which the dominant first response is incorrect). With more difficult anagrams, such as "theloacco," people did worse when aroused by the presence of others.

This explains, Zajonc further reasoned, why the arousal produced by working in front of an audience or alongside co-actors had similarly boosted performance on *simple* tasks (recall the fishing reels, simple multiplication problems, and chickens eating) and hindered performance on *difficult* tasks (learning new material, solving a maze, doing complex multiplication problems).

Suddenly seemingly contradictory results were unified by a general rule: *social arousal facilitates dominant responses*.

Zajonc's beautifully simple solution caused other psychologists to wonder, as did Thomas H. Huxley after reading Darwin's *On the Origin of Species*, "How extremely stupid not to have thought of that!"

But would the solution survive direct experimental tests? It did, across more than three hundred studies of more than twenty-five thousand people. Social arousal produced by others' presence led students to solve a simple maze more quickly and a complex one more slowly. Skilled student pool shooters, who had made 71 percent of their shots while being unobtrusively observed, made 80 percent when four people watched them. Unskilled pool shooters, who had made 36 percent of their shots while being unobtrusively observed, made only 25 percent when they knew they were being observed. And like those chickens, people scarf more food when eating with a group. (You, too?)

Well-practiced musicians, actors, and athletes also tend to excel when energized by an audience. For athletes, this contributes to the home advantage found in an analysis of more than a quarter million college and professional sports events—ranging from 56 percent winning by baseball home teams to 67 percent in soccer. So what happened during the pandemic—at "ghost matches" played before empty stadiums? The home advantage largely disappeared.

Home audiences are especially arousing because of *evaluation apprehension*: we care about what our friends and fans think. The presence of non-evaluating blindfolded people, or of someone facing away from us, does not arouse us or boost well-practiced responses.

Even so, said Zajonc, for us social animals the mere presence of someone is energizing. Merely jogging with someone gives a boost. The route somehow goes faster.

So, how might social distancing affect the experience of classroom, worship, and performance audiences? As athletic and theater directors understand, a packed audience radiates energy. For example, it creates a funny effect: fun shared with others is distinctly more energizing and, therefore, more fun. Jonathan Freedman and his colleagues demonstrated this with university students and science center visitors. A humorous tape or movie became all the funnier—and people more readily laughed and clapped—when they were seated close together.

Other researchers have confirmed this phenomenon of proximity-induced arousal. When densely packed in a small room, people have had higher pulse rates and blood pressure. They're more energized. And that helps explain my repeated observation that a class of thirty-five students crammed in a room that seats thirty-five is vastly livelier—and my jokes funnier—than when spread around a room that seats seventy.

Thus, I aim to maximize people's proximity and facial exposure to one another. When teaching thirty-five students in a room with extra chairs, I would arrive early, stack the extra chairs in the back, and group the just-needed chairs close together in arced rows. The difference, as surprisingly few teachers seem to appreciate, is huge. Worship leaders would likewise be well advised to eliminate unneeded pews to create a more densely packed, vibrant congregation, thus transforming lifeless singing into energized singing.

Although needed amid a pandemic, physical distancing sucks the energy from social experiences, while physical closeness ignites people power. So, for your next event, arrange the seating to barely accommodate everyone. Whether for concerts, worship, theater, or sports, a full house is a good house.

25

THE HAPPY SCIENCE OF
MICRO-FRIENDSHIPS

As Aristotle recognized long ago, we are social animals. "Without friends," he observed in *Nicomachean Ethics*, "no one would choose to live." Cut off from friends or family—alone in a foreign land, isolated during a pandemic, or separated by a death—people acutely feel their lost connections. Thanks to our distant ancestors surviving in groups that collectively hunted, shared, and protected, nature has endowed us with a powerful *need to belong*.

Our deeply social nature is revealed by the contribution of social support to our health and happiness. Folks who have close friends—people with whom they freely disclose their ups and downs, who rejoice with them over good news and commiserate over bad—live longer and more happily. In contrast, being ostracized, excluded, or shunned—your texts unanswered, your online friend ghosting you, others avoiding you—causes real emotional and physical pain. Loneliness is less a matter of being alone than of feeling ignored, dismissed, or uncared about. We are designed for relationships.

It's understandable, then, that with fewer pandemic-era face-to-face meetings, parties, and coffee catch-ups, people's mental health suffered. Separation from our nearest and dearest took an emotional toll. But what about those fleeting interactions—a brief chat in passing, a friendly exchange with the mail carrier, a casual conversation with the ride-share driver? Do these pandemic-diminished micro-connections also feed our souls? The consistent verdict of some inspiring social experiments is yes.

Bantering with a barista. The University of British Columbia researchers Gillian Sandstrom and Elizabeth Dunn offered patrons entering Starbucks a $5 gift card to participate in a simple experiment. After consenting, half were randomly assigned to be respectful but *efficient* when interacting with the barista ("have your money ready, and avoid unnecessary conversation"). The others were assigned to be *social* ("smile, make eye contact to establish a connection, and have a brief conversation"). When later exiting the store, those assigned to be social reported feeling more positive emotion, less negative emotion, and greater satisfaction with their Starbucks experience.

Reaching out to a stranger. In multiple experiments, the University of Chicago researchers Nicholas Epley and Juliana Schroeder similarly offered Chicago commuters a $5 gift card for completing a randomly assigned task: to (a) do as they would normally do on their train or bus, (b) sit in solitude, or (c) strike up a conversation with a stranger ("try to get to know your community neighbor this morning"). Although most people expected the attempted conversation would be awkward, the surprising outcome was positive: they were in a happier mood upon finishing their ride. Moreover, the intentional friendliness created an equally happy experience for both extraverts and introverts.

The delight of compliments received—and given. In five experiments, the University of Pennsylvania researchers Erica Boothby and Vanessa Bohns observed the unexpected power of compliments. In one, they instructed compliment givers to approach strangers, observe "something about them that you like" (often their hair or clothing), and compliment them on it. Although the compliment givers expected the compliment receivers would be a bit put off, perhaps feeling their own awkwardness, the consistent result was the opposite: the little act of kindness was warmly received. Even the compliment giver felt better afterward.

Engaging with a bus driver. At Turkey's Sabanci University, Gül Günaydin and colleagues wondered if greeting, thanking, or expressing good wishes to campus shuttle drivers would boost commuters' happiness. A survey revealed that those who routinely did so were happier. But maybe happy people are just friendlier? To pin down cause and effect, they experimented. They gave some commuters an envelope with instructions to do as Günaydin reports Turks normally do: to not speak with the driver. Others were asked to smile, make eye contact, and say something like "Thank you" or "Have a nice day." When later hopping off the bus, the friendly acting commuters felt happier. As Aesop long ago recognized (*The*

Lion and the Mouse), "No act of kindness, however small, is ever wasted."

The moral of the story: "pro-sociality" doesn't just brighten others' days; it brightens one's own. As the pandemic ends, and our facial expressions are no longer masked, we will surely savor our renewed connections—even our micro-connections.

I wondered, does the lesson of these studies ring true in my Facebook friends' everyday lives, as it does in mine? So I asked them, can you recall happy experiences of humanizing brief interactions—either as giver or as receiver?

Dozens of heartwarming replies flooded in.

Many recalled the happy results of reaching out to homeless people, grocery store clerks, tradespeople, taxi drivers, and fellow hikers, campers, or dog walkers. Teachers reported, during the pandemic, missing "the short conversations outside of class time—in hallways, in the lunch line, at the door on the way into or out of school . . . the little blessings [that] enrich my day and my membership in the community."

Others recalled how, with repeated brief encounters, miniature but meaningful relationships arose. Repeated micro-interactions with restaurant servers, corner shop owners, or pharmacists grew into fondness: "On our daily walk past a hotel to our Tokyo train station we got to 'know' a friendly bellhop on a first name basis, with updates on her life. She would often run out and wave most enthusiastically greeting us."

Some noted the prevalence of micro-interactions in certain cultures. A friend reported that in Malawi "we had grown used to these kinds of micro friendships" as people exchange pleasantries with passersby on the street and with the vegetable and fruit sellers. "If they have their babies with them you greet them, too. Eventually you see that the baby is now in school and there is another one on the way, so you feel you have gotten to know them through a series of small exchanges over the years. When we left Malawi to return to the U.S. our daughter noticed the difference. She asked us, 'Have I disappeared?' When we asked why she said, 'No one greets me!'"

Others were inspired by *observing* micro-kindnesses, such as from a spouse who engages in a "spray of random acts and words of kindness"—given to clerks, delivery people, or the adjacent person at a concert "with a smile and chat that leaves them smiling in return." Another admired a friend who "will often meet someone—perhaps just for a moment—and take the time to tell them something strikingly wonderful about themselves."

My friends also recalled *receiving* kindhearted gestures from strangers—from a 7-Eleven store owner having dog treats ready, a Red Cross nurse giving infusions with a personal conversation, or a fellow airplane passenger who, on landing, complimented a mom of three young children: "'You were very patient.' Music to my ears and heart."

One woman, stressed by managing a clinic at the pandemic's beginning, stopped by Walmart to console herself with "a family-sized bag of chocolate." The cashier, "a young 20-something man, asked me if I'd come all the way to the store just for chocolate. I said yes, it had been a bad day. He then asked me why and I just burst into tears. His genuine interest and compassion were so validating and humanizing that the floodgates broke. He probably thought he made my day worse . . . but he really made my day better and I think I will never forget the kindness of this young guy toward a hot mess 40-something mom."

Sometimes micro-kindnesses are, indeed, long remembered. One man recalled, "When I was a college student, I used to smile and greet the only other dark-skinned Mexican on campus (a small California college). The other students used to mock him for his [older] age, quirky personality, and appearance. We never had classes together so I never really got to know him. But at graduation he approached me tearfully and thanked me for my frequent smiles and greetings. He told me that often it was the only kindness he would experience for long periods at the college, and that it helped him get through."

Another told of seeing an older, white-haired man buying roses and chocolates. "I smiled at him and commented, 'How nice! Someone special will love receiving those on Valentine's Day.' He turned to me, made intense eye contact, and said, 'They are for my wife. I am giving them to her today. We just found out that she has leukemia.' Then we just gazed at each other for a few seconds, searching each other's souls, it felt like. He wanted, needed a response. I asked God for words, and to perceive exactly what he needed. I finally said from my own heart, 'Every woman dreams of finding someone like you to love her forever, no matter what.' It happened so fast.

The gratitude that swept over his face melted into a smile. He really needed someone to see him and hear him, exactly where he was in that moment, I think. 'I'll take good care of her,' he said as he left, his voice stronger. 'I know you will,' I said back, lifting a silent prayer of thanksgiving."

26

HOW TO MAKE AND SUSTAIN
FRIENDSHIPS

We are social animals. We flourish when supported by close relationships. When we find a supportive confidant, we feel joy. As Pope Francis has said, "Everyone's existence is deeply tied to that of others."

How many others? About 150 people, contends the retired Oxford evolutionary psychologist Robin Dunbar. He defends that number—Dunbar's number, as it has become known—from studies of human networks ranging from Neolithic and medieval villages to modern wedding invitation and Christmas card lists. Our friendship layers, he adds, typically begin with a core of about five intimate shoulder-to-cry-on friends—people we're in touch with "at least once a week and feel close to." From analyzing time diaries and phone data, Dunbar reports that these folks represent about 40 percent of our total social time. In the next relationship layer, we tend to have about ten more close friends with whom we're in touch at least monthly, and in whom we invest an additional 20 percent of our social time (thus about 60 percent of our social effort typically focuses on about fifteen people). Beyond those are another thirty-five or so "party friends" whom we may connect with at least once every six months. The total Dunbar number, 150, adds those we're in touch with at least annually—"what you might call the wedding/bar mitzvah/ funeral group—the people that would turn up to your once-in-a-lifetime events."

If psychological science has proven anything, it's that friends matter. Feeling liked, supported, and encouraged by close friends and family enables better sleep, reduces blood pressure, and even boosts immune functioning. Compared with socially isolated or lonely folks, those socially connected are at less risk of premature death. As the writer of Ecclesiastes surmised, "Woe to one who is alone and falls and does not have another to help."

Longing for approval, acceptance, and love, Americans spend $86 billion annually on cosmetics, fragrances, and personal care products, and billions more on clothes, hairstyling, and diets. Is that money well spent? And what else—or more greatly—determines the impressions we make and the relationships we hope to form and sustain? Decades of research offer some simple predictors.

Proximity. Our social ecology matters. We tend to like those nearby—those who sit near us in class, at work, in worship. Our nearest become our dearest as we befriend or marry people who live in the same town, attend the same school, share the same mail room, or visit the same coffee shop. Mere exposure breeds liking. Familiar feels friendly. Customary is comfortable. So look around.

Similarity. Hundreds of experiments confirm and reconfirm that likeness leads to liking (and thus the challenge of welcoming the benefits of social diversity). The more similar another's attitudes, beliefs, interests, politics, income, and on and on, the more disposed we are to like the person and to stay connected. And the more dissimilar another's attitudes, the greater the odds of disliking. Opposites retract.

Although proximity and similarity help bonds form, we needn't be constrained by the small circle of our existing relationships. Venturing to new schools, new jobs, new places can entail new proximities and enable us to discover kindred spirits in unexpected places. Moreover, other influences also feed and sustain relationships.

Equity. One key to relationship endurance is equity, which occurs when friends or lovers perceive that they receive in proportion to what they give. When two people share their time and possessions, when they give and receive support in equal measure, and when they care equally about each other, their prospects for long-term friendship or love are bright.

A relationship's beginning often involves social ping-pong. I invite you to my party; then you reciprocate. You lend me your class notes; then I lend you mine. But over time, the tit-for-tat exchange subsides, as each friend or partner invests in the other about as much as he or she receives. Indeed, in a deepening relationship, the social psychologists Margaret

Clark and Judson Mills found, people *avoid* quick exchanges. We don't want to keep score by instantly replaying favors.

Still, over the long term, equity matters. Where people receive over time in proportion to what they give, friendship or love commonly endures. If one person disproportionately benefits, the over-benefited one may feel guilt and the under-benefited one will likely feel irritated. Show marriage researchers a relationship with perceived total inequity—in housekeeping, cooking, parenting, and provisioning—and they will likely show you a distressed marriage. As one Pew Research Center report concluded, "I like hugs. I like kisses. But what I really love is help with the dishes."

Self-disclosure. Relationships also grow closer and stronger as we share our likes and dislikes, our joys and hurts, our dreams and worries. In the dance of friendship or love, one reveals a little and the other reciprocates. And then the first reveals more, and on and on. As the relationship progresses from small talk to things that matter, the increasing self-disclosure can elicit liking, which unleashes further self-disclosure. "When I am with my friend," observed the Roman sage Seneca, I am "as much at liberty to speak anything as to think it."

The social psychologist Arthur Aron and his colleagues experimented with the bonding power of self-disclosure. They invited student pairs to become acquainted in response to forty-five minutes of either small-talk questions ("What was your high school like?") or progressively more self-disclosing questions ("What is the greatest accomplishment of your life?" "When did you last cry?"). By the experiment's end, those who experienced the escalating self-disclosure felt much closer to their conversation partners than did those who engaged in small talk.

People appreciate the chance to open up to another and then to receive the other's trust by being similarly open with us. People feel better on days when they have had a self-disclosing conversation. And those whose days more often include deep or substantive conversations tend to be happier, as Matthias Mehl and his research team observed after equipping students with recorders that snatched thirty-second conversational snippets over four days. Except when it is too much too soon, self-disclosure feeds friendships and feels good.

Mindful of the benefits of equity and mutual self-disclosure, we can monitor our conversations: Are we listening as much as we are talking? And are we drawing others out as much as we are disclosing about ourselves?

Some people are especially skilled "openers." They more easily elicit intimate disclosures, even from those who normally don't reveal much. Such people tend to be empathic listeners. During conversation, they maintain attentive facial expressions and eye contact that displays interest and enjoyment. In his classic *How to Win Friends and Influence People*, Dale Carnegie offered familiar but true advice. To win friends, he advised, "become genuinely interested in other people . . . You can make more friends in two months by being interested in them, than in two years by making them interested in you." Thus, "Be a good listener. Encourage others to talk about themselves."

The magic ratio. It's no surprise that studies of thousands of couples find that unhappy couples criticize, put down, command, and disagree, while happy couples more often compliment, approve, agree, and assent. Knowing that all relationships offer a mix of criticism and affirmation, the marriage researcher John Gottman studied the nature of that mix in failing and successful marriages. He invited couples to revisit a conflict, and observed their interactions. Then he followed their marriage over nine years. In thriving marriages, he found, positive interactions (complimenting, smiling, touching, laughing) outnumbered negative ones (criticisms, insults, sarcasm) by at least a five-to-one ratio—the "magic relationship ratio."

In our other relationships, too—perhaps you have noticed—an insult makes us feel worse than a compliment makes us feel good. As Roy Baumeister and others remind us, "Bad is stronger than good." It takes multiple kind words to equal the impact of one hurting word. Long after a kindness has been forgotten, the hurt from a cruelty lingers.

Gottman understands. Show him a relationship that has five or more positive communications and interactions for every negative one, and he will show you a healthy relationship.

Being reminded of the magic ratio always makes me ponder: Am I, in my various relationships, offering words of appreciation, affection, and interest at least five times more often than I criticize or scorn?

27

NARCISSISM:
THE GRANDIOSE SELF

Self-serving bias (perceiving and explaining ourselves favorably) is natural and normal, albeit occasionally problematic. But what are the roots and fruits of *extreme* self-serving bias, *narcissism*?

Is narcissism just a cover for insecurity or low self-esteem? It seems not, because on various self-esteem measures, narcissistic people routinely score high.

But are narcissists' inflated sense of self a mask that covers their deep-down sense of inferiority? Again, no. When playing a computer game in which they must quickly press a key to match the word "me" with both positive words (such as "good," "great," "wonderful") and negative words ("awful," "bad," "terrible"), narcissists respond faster when associating themselves with positive rather than negative words. Deep down, narcissists truly think of themselves as awesome.

To study narcissists' reactions to criticism, the social psychologists Brad Bushman and Roy Baumeister had undergraduate volunteers write essays and receive fake feedback. When they were praised ("great essay!"), those who scored high on a narcissism scale by agreeing with statements such as "If I ruled the world, it would be a better place," or "I think I am a special person," were, as you would expect, pleased. But if they were criticized ("This is one of the worst essays I've read!"), the narcissists, who crave adulation, were much more likely than those low in self-esteem to retaliate, by pushing a button that blasted aversive noise at the one who criticized them.

So, too, in a classroom setting, where the self-inflated narcissists were especially likely to assign a bad grade to a classmate who had previously criticized them. When receiving *public* criticism—when their public image of superiority is punctured—narcissists become especially likely to lash out. Narcissists may be charming, but only until you cross them.

In studies of human development, narcissists have often come from homes where parents believed their children deserved special treatment. Many modern parents have conveyed just that message, which helps explain the rise in U.S. students' narcissism scores, as reported by my colleague Jean Twenge. Other parents, who simply display love and kindness, tend not to have narcissistic children. So, instead of repeatedly telling their children how special they are, parents might more simply tell them they are loved. When it comes to nurturing non-defensive adults, parental warmth beats parental praising.

People with high self-esteem typically value achievement and relationships. Narcissists prize achievement but care less about relationships. Early on in social settings, narcissists often charm people with their outgoing and flamboyant personalities. They tend to be very active on social media with status updates and tweets, and to amass many friends and followers. In two studies, narcissism has even been associated with becoming a reality TV star.

But with time, their self-centeredness and volatility wear thin. In one study, those scoring high in narcissism often emerged as a leader among students they hadn't previously met. But after further group meetings, their popularity declined as group members came to realize that the leader did not prioritize their interests. Over time, narcissists' thin-skinned antagonism and willingness to cheat others contribute to their declining reputation. Narcissists (who are mostly men) also tend to take a game-playing approach to romance and, more than other men, may seek sexual hookups or be sexually coercive.

For all these reasons, psychological scientists now include narcissism in "the Dark Triad" of negative traits, alongside Machiavellianism (manipulativeness) and antisocial psychopathy. The narcissism/Machiavellianism/psychopathy trio of traits tends to coexist in people who are callous, self-promoting, and remorseless (rather than agreeable, compassionate, and empathic). These folks are not your favorite co-workers or romantic partners.

So, does the constellation of narcissism traits remind you of anyone? Someone—likely a man—with an inflated ego? An eagerness to exaggerate his own superiority? A need to be admired? A tendency to monopolize conversations? A readiness to lash out when questioned or criticized? A willingness to demean and bully others? A propensity to lie? A lack of empathy? A tendency to exploit, cheat, and then discard others? A history of sexually self-gratifying behavior? And, in the end, a declining reputation and ultimate rejection by others?

PART III

WHAT IN THE WORLD?

28

HOW NATURE AND NURTURE FORM US

A recent experience illustrates a big lesson of longitudinal studies (studies that follow lives across time). My personal method was simple:

1. Observation 1: Attend a small college, living on campus and closely observing my friends.
2. Intervening experience: Let fifty years of life unfold, taking us all to varied places.
3. Observation 2: Meet and talk with these friends again, at a college reunion.

Time and again, researchers have documented the remarkable stability of emotionality, intelligence, and personality across decades of life. "As at age seven, so at seventy," says a Jewish proverb.

And so it was with my friends (with names changed to protect identities). Thoughtful, serious Joe was still making earnest pronouncements. Driven, status-conscious Louise continues to visibly excel. Exuberant Mark could still talk for ten minutes while hardly catching a breath. Gentle, kind Laura was still sensitive and kindhearted. The mischievous prankster George still evinced an edgy, impish spirit. Smiling, happy Joanne still readily grinned and laughed. I was amazed: half a century, and yet everyone seemed the same person who walked off that graduation stage.

Behavior geneticists would not be surprised. They have gifted us with two stunning findings—the most shocking findings in all of psychological science. Together these findings have overturned what I formerly believed about the environment's power to shape personality.

The first finding—dramatically illustrated by the studies of identical twins separated near birth—is the heritability of personality and intelligence. In study after study in country after country, genetically identical twins are (when compared with fraternal twins who share the same home and school) much more alike in the Big Five personality traits— openness, conscientiousness, agreeableness, neuroticism, and extraversion.

Indeed, as is well known by now, the striking similarities of identical twins extend to those separated at birth and then reared without knowledge of each other. In personality, intelligence, and various physical traits, they are nearly as alike as the same person tested twice.

Ah, but might identical twins have similar personalities not just because of their shared genes but also because their environments respond to their similar *looks*? If only there were people who similarly look alike but don't share the same genes.

Happily there *are* unrelated look-alikes—non-twin "doppelgängers" identified by the Montreal photographer François Brunelle, who for many years has been collecting (through the media and his website) black-and-white photos of look-alikes. The California State University, Fullerton, twin researcher Nancy Segal seized this opportunity to give personality and self-esteem inventories to twenty-three pairs of Brunelle's human look-alikes. Unlike identical twins, look-alikes do *not* have notably similar traits and self-esteem. In a follow-up study with Jamie Graham and Ulrich Ettinger, Segal replicated that finding and reported that the look-alikes (unlike the soul-mate biological twin look-alikes) do not develop special bonds after meeting their doppelgänger. So, genes' influence on basic traits exceeds any influence of the environment's response to our looks.

The second finding—dramatically illustrated by the dissimilar personalities and talents of adoptive children raised in the same home and neighborhood—is the modest influence of their "shared environment." In personality traits such as agreeableness and extraversion, adoptees are more similar to their *biological* parents than to their caregiving adoptive parents.

The behavior geneticist Robert Plomin puts it baldly: "We would essentially be the same person if we had been adopted at birth and raised in a different family." To the developmental psychologist Sandra Scarr, this implied that "parents should be given less credit for kids who turn out great and blamed less for kids who don't." Rather than try to remold their children, parents might better relax and love their children's personalities and intellects as they are.

On the other hand, studies of impoverishment during the preschool years, of epigenetic constraints on genetic expression, and of family influences on attitudes, values, and beliefs remind us the environment (including adoption) matters, too. Even the significant peer influences on attitudes, accents, and allegiances are swayed by parents' neighborhood and school choices. Genetic dispositions are always expressed in particular environments. Nature and nurture, like warp and woof, together weave the fabric of our human experience.

The greater malleability of attitudes and ideals has been evident with my college friends. My formerly kindred-spirited dorm mates had moved in different directions . . . some now expressing concerns about cultural moral decay and big government, and others now passionate about justice and support for gays and lesbians. Before they opened their mouths, I had no idea which was going to be which.

And isn't that the life experience of each of us—that our development is a story of both genetically influenced stability and socially influenced change? And thank goodness for both. Stability provides our identity across time, while our potential for change enables us to grow with experience and to hope for a brighter future.

People do, selectively, appreciate the behavior genetics lesson. A University of Minnesota team surveyed a thousand Americans regarding their beliefs about the relative contributions of genes and environments to various traits. Liberals more than conservatives saw genetics having a strong influence on psychiatric disorders and sexual orientation. Conservatives more often saw a strong genetic influence on intelligence and musical ability, which they viewed as largely "born that way" rather than advantaged by opportunity.

Parents, too, gain a sense of heredity's formative power. Most folks, it has been said, believe in the shaping power of environmental nurture—until they have their second child. That pretty well sums up the Minnesota survey result. The researchers report that "educated mothers with multiple children" were particularly cognizant of the heritability of traits, adding, "Parents, after all, have the ability to observe firsthand the results of an empirical experiment on the heritability of human traits in their own home. They can see that their children resemble them along multiple dimensions; furthermore, a parent of multiple children can see how the shared environment does not necessarily make them alike."

That has been my wife's and my experience as parents of three children who—after we shuffled our gene decks and dealt each a hand—share some of our traits, but who were distinct individuals right out of the womb. And perhaps that's your experience, too, as you compare your children, or observe your own or others' siblings?

29

THE WONDER OF WALKING (AND SINGING): SYNCHRONIZED SPIRITS

magine that you and a colleague (or spouse) have been at odds. You have argued and fought, each trying to persuade the other. Alas, there has been no meeting of the minds. What might you do next to create an opportunity for conflict resolution?

To "put behind" you where you have been stuck, to "move on" from your standstill, to "get beyond" your impasse, one simple, practical strategy is literally to take steps forward—*to go for a walk*. Christine Webb, Maya Rossignac-Milon, and E. Tory Higgins contend that "walking together can facilitate both the intra- and interpersonal pathways to conflict resolution."

The idea grows naturally from Higgins's studies of "embodied cognition," which is the influence of people's bodily sensations and movements on their judgments and preferences. In creative experiments, researchers have observed:

- *Wobbly seat, wobbly relationships.* Sitting at a wobbly desk and chair made others' relationships seem less stable.
- *Warm room, warm people.* On a warm day or in a warm room, people often felt more warm and friendly.
- *Hard chair, hard on crime.* Sitting on a hard rather than soft chair, people recommended harsher sentences for criminals and cheats.
- *Hard ball, hard politics.* If holding a hard ball rather than a soft ball, people were more likely to guess someone to be a Republican rather than a Democrat, or a physicist rather than a historian.
- *Head high, spirits high.* Striding with head high and shoulders back (rather than slumped and shuffling), people feel more confident.

We think from within a body. The brain networks that process our body's sensations communicate with the brain networks that enable our thinking.

Walking also reduces stress, report the embodied cognition researchers. Walking boosts mood. It supports creativity. Throughout history, walking has freed the mind for thinking. For Nietzsche, "All truly great thoughts are achieved by walking." "My mind only works with my legs," said Rousseau. For Emerson, walking was "gymnastics for the mind." "I have walked myself into my best thoughts," reflected Kierkegaard. "Kant, Einstein, Mozart, and even Steve Jobs were all said to take routine walks," report Webb and her colleagues.

At the interpersonal level, walking does more. In contrast to face-to-face staring during a conflict, walking softens the boundary between self and other. Without eye contact, people may feel more comfortable with self-disclosure. Walking embodies forward movement. Even with strangers in a laboratory, side-by-side walking increases spontaneous coordination of mental states, perspectives, and goals. Walkers' synchronous movements, as they jointly attend to their environment and coordinate their steps, increase mutual rapport and empathy.

In experiments, those who mimic another's movements report liking the other more. Empathic mimicking—as when a listener nods their head or winces when you do—fosters fondness. We not only mirror the movements of those we like, we like those who mirror our own. Biologists who study herding in mammals and synchronized movements in bird flocks and fish schools speculate on the deep adaptive functions of behavioral synchrony. Perhaps for our early ancestors, too, theorizes the British psychologist Liam Cross, synchronized movements helped strengthen bonds, signal cooperation, and display strength.

If, indeed, synchronous walking increases rapport and pro-sociality—if, as we've noted, our motions influence our emotions—then might there be a similar effect of synchronized line dancing? Of martial drills? Of jointly clapping our applause? Even of singing? Does group singing help unify a diverse audience?

The question crossed my mind as the folk singer Peter Yarrow (of Peter, Paul and Mary) rose near the beginning of a recent small group retreat of diverse people and invited us to join him in singing "Music Speaks Louder Than Words." Yarrow has spent his career—from the civil rights and antiwar movements of the 1960s to today—in engaging audiences in synchronized singing of pro-social poetry.

What do you think? Do synchronized walking, dancing, and group singing have psychological effects? Can they lift us beyond where words, in isolation, can take us? To literally put us in sync with others?

30

WISE INTERVENTIONS CAN CHANGE LIVES

P sychology's archives are filled with well-meaning, well-funded endeavors that were meant to change lives for the better but that, regrettably, made no difference. Yet now comes news of some brief, evidence-based interventions that offer surprising benefits. But first the bad news:

In one huge study, five hundred Massachusetts boys deemed at risk for delinquency were, by the toss of a coin, assigned either to a no-intervention control condition or to a five-year treatment program. In addition to twice-a-month visits from counselors, the boys in the treatment program received academic tutoring, medical attention, and family assistance. They also participated in community programs, such as the Boy Scouts.

When Joan McCord located 97 percent of the participants some thirty years later, many offered glowing testimonials: Were it not for the program, "I would probably be in jail"; "My life would have gone the other way"; or "I think I would have ended up in a life of crime." Indeed, even among "difficult" predelinquent boys, 66 percent developed no juvenile crime record.

But the same was true of their control counterparts, 70 percent of whom had no juvenile record. Alas, the glowing testimonials had been unintentionally deceiving. The program had no beneficial effect.

More recently, other endeavors—the national Scared Straight program to tame teenage violence, the police-promoted DARE antidrug effort, Critical Incident Stress Debriefing for trauma victims, and numerous weight-reduction, pedophile rehabilitation, and sexual reorientation efforts—have also been found ineffectual or even harmful.

Is this because genes fix our traits—minimizing our malleability? (Remember those dozens of identical twins who, though raised separately, are still amazingly similar.) To be sure, genes do matter. The most comprehensive review of twin studies—more than three thousand such studies encompassing 14.6 million twins—found that "across all traits the reported heritability [individual differences attributable to genes] is 49 percent." That is substantial, yet it leaves room for willpower, beliefs, and social influence as well. Body weight, for example, is genetically influenced, but diet and exercise also matter.

Given the guiding power of our heredity and the failure of many large-scale efforts to help people flourish, I am stunned by the seeming successes of brief "wise interventions" ("wise" in the sense of being savvy about how our beliefs and assumptions influence us). Why does a one-hour intervention sometimes outperform a five-year intervention? Consider three examples.

1. At-risk middle school students given a "growth mindset"—by being taught that the brain, like a muscle, grows with use—achieved better grades because they "saw effort as a virtue, because effort helps to develop ability."

2. Entering minority college students who experienced a one-hour session explaining the normality of the worry that they didn't belong (with reassuring stories from older peers) achieved higher grades over the next three years, closing the racial GPA gap from 0.29 to 0.14, and had greater life and career satisfaction three to five years after college.

3. When paraprofessionals helped at-risk new mothers understand their baby's fussing, the moms were less likely to think of themselves as bad mothers, and first-year child abuse was reduced from 23 to 4 percent.

Two leading researchers, Gregory Walton and Timothy Wilson, recently reviewed 325 interventions. Their conclusion: helping people reframe the meaning of their experiences can promote their long-term flourishing. As Walton and Wilson have explained, wise interventions focus on how people make sense of or interpret themselves, other people, or a social situation. When a new parent struggles to calm a crying baby, does she worry that she might be a "bad mom" or that her child might be a "bad baby"? When a student receives critical academic feedback, does he worry that his teacher might have judged him as unintelligent? When a new college student feels lonely or isolated on campus, does she wonder, "Can people like me belong here?" When groups are in conflict, people may wonder, "Can groups ever change?"

People's answers to such questions drive their behavior, say Walton and Wilson. "If the student infers that his teacher thinks he is dumb, he is less likely to talk with the teacher after school about something he doesn't understand. He may even act out in class. And that could set in motion a negative cycle with the teacher—that prevents both him and his teacher from achieving their shared goals over time."

Or if a college student feels she doesn't belong on her campus, she may shy away from going to office hours and meeting a professor. But if a brief intervention could help her feel she belongs, then she might meet the prof who could become a mentor.

So, helping people draw helpful meanings at key times—when the twig that forms the tree is being bent—can enhance achievement at school, health at home, or overall well-being. For example, despite college administrators' frustrated past efforts to increase at-risk students' college success, a brief intervention just before their coming to campus can make a difference. New minority students who read older minority students' stories of initially feeling like a fish out of water, until acclimating, have persisted to achieve better grades and more campus engagement.

Like clay, conclude Walton and Wilson, meanings are malleable at transitional times, and thereafter become fixed, for better or worse. Wise interventions are transformational when, at such times, they help frame people's interpretations about their abilities, their relationships, or their parenting.

31

FAILURE AND FLOURISHING

There's a big difference between my world and yours," I've explained to my college's basketball coaches. "Your victories and defeats are there for all to see. We scholars only announce our victories."

Moreover, as most academics and many businesspeople will confirm, our careers resemble an iceberg, with our victories visible above our beneath-the-surface failures. Our CVs and websites are like many people's idyllic social media feeds—misleadingly suggesting a trajectory of success.

So why not make our setbacks more visible? asked the researcher Melanie Stefan in a 2010 *Nature* letter. Instead of scholars hiding their failures and trumpeting their successes (which surely, she notes, can leave colleagues "feeling alone and dejected" when their work gets rejected), why not "compile an 'alternative' CV of failures"?

Stefan inspired the Stockholm University economist Johannes Haushofer to offer on his website both a customary CV and a CV of Failures. The neuroscientist Bradley Voytek likewise appends to the end of his impressive CV his failed graduate school and job applications, his many unsuccessful award and grant applications, and the multiple rejections that preceded many of his publications.

Rejection is the apt title of John White's obscure little 1982 book that recounts one story after another of famed works that achieved acclaim or even Nobel Prizes after repeated rejections. White reports that Dr. Seuss was rejected by some two dozen publishers, and that one of the seven publishers that rejected *The Tale of Peter Rabbit* scornfully said that the tale "smelled like rotting carrots."

Such stories continue to accumulate: J. K. Rowling's initial rejection by "loads" of publishers, the *New Yorker* cartoonist Tom Toro finally making the magazine on his 610th try, and Peter Ratcliffe winning the 2019 Nobel Prize in Medicine for work that *Nature* had rejected.

In the spirit of Melanie Stefan's admonition to be more disclosing, let me admit that I set a literary agent's house record by having a trade book proposal rejected by thirty-six publishers. If only this story had a happy ending. Alas, when the book was eventually published, it sold little. In hindsight, those thirty-six publishers hadn't misjudged the book's public appeal.

But then I also recall, some years ago, feeling deflated when *Today's Education* rejected my critique of the labeling and segregation of "gifted" (and, by implication, ungifted) children. After submitting the paper to half a dozen other periodicals, which likewise rejected it, I noticed that *Today's Education* had a new editorial team. When I resubmitted the revised and now co-authored piece to *Today's Education*, they unhesitatingly published it, gave permission for its reprinting in newspapers and magazines, and invited me to write more.

The dismissal of our work extends to searing reviews. In my experience, colleagues and students, even when offering criticism, are overwhelmingly kind and encouraging. But I should admit that any marketing tributes you might have read of my work are partly offset by comments you haven't seen, such as "Based on my reading of the chapter, I would not adopt the book. If someone asked me about the book, I would tell them not to use it. Based on my reading of this chapter, I would not adopt any book by Myers and would tell others not to adopt a book by Myers."

Such experiences of criticism extend to every teacher's end-of-semester student evaluations. As one senior colleague said when offering teaching advice, "Realize that in teaching, as in life, two things are certain: (1) you're going to make a fool of yourself at some point, and (2) you're going to have your heart broken." As any teacher (or romantic partner) can vouch, the emotional impact of negative and positive feedback is asymmetrical: a single criticism deflates us more than a single compliment elates us. If, as John Gottman has long reported, a five-to-one positive-to-negative ratio is needed to sustain a marriage, a similar ratio is surely required to sustain a teacher.

Many a teacher can recall feeling buoyed by students' mostly affirming evaluations, then abruptly deflated by a dagger or two—like this anonymous feedback from one of my students:

QUESTION: What did you find beneficial about this course?
ANSWER: Nothing

QUESTION: If you think that the course could be improved,
what would you suggest?
ANSWER: End the course

QUESTION: What advice would you give to a friend who is
planning to take this course?
ANSWER: Don't

Ouch! I have given talks to colleagues about lessons I've
learned professing psychology, explaining some secrets of
success, but also disclosing these and other rejections and
disparagements I've experienced. Time and again, it's the
confessions of failure and disapproval that people later report
appreciating. "That was so helpful to hear—that it's not just
me!" When we're exposed only to others' triumphs, we can,
by comparison, feel mediocre. It helps to know that others
experience the slings of failure and arrows of scorn.

From my own and others' experiences of criticism and
rejection, I draw three additional lessons:

First, *welcome criticism*. In his 1957 book, *Psychological
Research*, the great memory researcher Benton Underwood
explained,

The rejection of my own manuscripts has a sordid
aftermath: (a) One day of depression; (b) one day of
utter contempt for the editor and his accomplices;

(c) one day of decrying the conspiracy against letting Truth be published; (d) one day of fretful ideas about changing my profession; (e) one day of re-evaluating the manuscript in view of the editor's comments followed by the conclusion that I was lucky it wasn't accepted.

Second, *if your aim is worthy, persist.* Be mindful that to teach, to write, or to lead is to expose yourself to criticism, to contempt, even to attack. Learn what you can, but do not let criticism and rejection intimidate you into submission. And know that as feedback accumulates across your life experience, criticism will lose its power to deflate your spirit, even as praise loses its power to inflate your ego.

Third, *to succeed, you must be willing to fail.* "Twenty-six times I've been trusted to take the game-winning shot—and missed," said Michael Jordan in a 1997 Nike ad. "I've failed over and over and over again in my life. And that is why I succeed." Life has us on a partial reinforcement schedule. What one reviewer thinks is pointless, another may find pioneering. What one critic finds "too cute," another may find "refreshingly witty." As Skinner's occasionally reinforced rats and pigeons taught us long ago, *you don't get pellets unless you press the bar.*

32

DEATH IS TERRIFYING TO CONTEMPLATE, EXCEPT FOR THOSE WHO ARE DYING

We humans have an overwhelming fear of death. That's the core assumption of "terror management theory." When confronted with reminders of our mortality, the theory presumes, we display self-protective emotional and cognitive responses. Made to think about dying, we self-defensively cling tightly to our worldviews and prejudices.

On the assumption that dying is terrifying—that death is the great enemy to be avoided at all costs—medicine devotes enormous resources to avoiding death, even to extending life by a matter of hours. And should we be surprised? I love being alive and hope to have miles of purposeful life to go before I sleep.

So, do we have the worst of life yet to come? Are we right to view life's end with despair? Consider two psychological science principles:

1. *The stability of well-being.* Across the life span, people mostly report being satisfied and happy with their lives. Subjective well-being does not plummet in the post-sixty-five years. In later life, stresses also become fewer, and life becomes less of an emotional roller coaster.

2. *Human resilience.* More than most people assume, humans adapt to change. Good events—even a lottery win—elate us for a time, but then we adapt and our normal mix of emotions returns. Bad events—such as becoming paralyzed in an accident—devastate us, but only for a while. Both pleasures and tragedies have a surprisingly short half-life. As I face my increasing deafness, the reality of resilience is reassuring.

And now comes a third striking finding: *dying is less traumatic than people suppose.* Amelia Goranson and her colleagues examined

A. the blog posts of terminally ill cancer and ALS patients (obtained via Google search), and
B. the last words of death row inmates before their execution (as recorded by the Texas Department of Criminal Justice since 1982).

But first they asked others to simulate those posts and words. When asked to imagine the posts of those facing death, people typically expressed despair, anger, or anxiety. An example:

I feel like my body has betrayed me, like I am not who I thought I was. I have a growth inside of me, an alien, an intruder of the worst kind. And it will continue to grow and overtake me, from the inside out. Slowly but quickly at the same time. At this point all I can express is my shock and betrayal. I hope to come to find a place of acceptance and peace, but right now I honestly just feel like going to sleep and never having to wake up again.

More than expected—and increasingly as death approached—the actual words of the dying expressed social connection, love, meaning, and faith. The first of 2,632 posts by those terminally ill illustrates this point:

It feels like the end is getting closer. Connected full time to morphine pump, but pain is still unrelenting, especially in shoulder. Breathing harder. All water and nutrition now through gravity bags—drip, drip, drip. Need assistance for every movement.

Surrounded here by so much love and care I feel I am ready for the next step. I have no regrets at all—I have had a full life, touched and been touched by such wonderful family and friends.

So if there is to be a final lesson for me it is that love is the ultimate gift—love and honesty.

I am so grateful for the messages of support I have received from readers of this blog. And for all the wonderful friends, especially fellow PALS, I have met here. I hope my writing has provided you with some insight and strength with your own challenges—ALS or whatever.

I will soon be at peace, my struggles past. But I will be here in spirit to help strengthen each of you in your lives. So if you hear a little voice whispering "Love," know it is me.

Likewise, people expected death row inmates to offer reflections such as this:

I am feeling worse about myself and my actions than about anything or at any time in my life. If I was given the opportunity to go back and do things differently, I would do so. I ask for the forgiveness of those I have hurt and pray to God I may make up for the harm I have done.

But this actual blog post by an inmate on death row was more typical:

Yes. I just want to let you all know that I appreciate the love and support over the years. I will see you when you get there. Keep your heads up. To all the fellows on the Row, the same thing. Keep your head up and continue to fight. Same thing to all my pen friends and other friends, I love you all. I can taste it.

Goranson and her colleagues presume (though it remains to be shown) that the same acceptance and positivity will be exhibited by those dying at the more expected time on the social clock—very late in life, when people (despite stereotypes of grumpy old folks) tend to focus on the positive. And so it was for the civil rights legend and congressman John Lewis, who submitted these op-ed words two days before his 2020 death:

> While my time here has now come to an end, I want you to know that in the last days and hours of my life you inspired me. You filled me with hope about the next chapter of the great American story . . .
>
> When historians pick up their pens to write the story of the 21st century, let them say that it was your generation who laid down the heavy burdens of hate at last and that peace finally triumphed over violence, aggression and war. So I say to you, walk with the wind, brothers and sisters, and let the spirit of peace and the power of everlasting love be your guide.

The moral to the story (in the researchers' words): "Death is more positive than people expect: Meeting the grim reaper may not be as grim as it seems."

33

DO PLACES WITH MORE IMMIGRANTS EXHIBIT GREATER ACCEPTANCE OR GREATER FEAR OF IMMIGRANTS?

Mexican immigrants, President Trump repeatedly told his approving base, are "bringing drugs. They're bringing crime. They're rapists." At a West Virginia rally, he highlighted Mollie Tibbetts's accused "illegal alien" killer as a vivid example. Hence the wish to "build a wall"—to keep out those who, we are told, would exploit Americans and take their jobs.

Setting aside the fearmongering's inaccuracy (undocumented immigrants are underrepresented in prisons), consider a different question: Who believes it? Is it people who live in regions with a greater number of unauthorized immigrants and who have suffered the presumed crime, conflict, and competition?

At a Sydney symposium on social psychology, Christian Unkelbach of the University of Cologne reported an intriguing finding: In Germany, anti-immigrant views are strongest in the states with *fewest* immigrants. Across Germany's sixteen states, intentions to vote for the right-wing Alternative für Deutschland (Alternative for Germany) were greatest in states with the *fewest* asylum applications.

I wondered, might a similar pattern—which another German research team has replicated—emerge in the United States? To find out, I combined two data sets:

1. A 2016 Pew report provided the percentage of unauthorized immigrants in each state's population.
2. A 2016 PRRI "American Values" report provided state-by-state data on immigrant acceptance.

Voilà! In the United States, too, the presence of more immigrants predicts greater state-level *acceptance* of immigrants. And a smaller immigrant population predicts greater fear of immigrants. For example, West Virginia, with the lowest unauthorized immigrant proportion, also is the least immigrant supportive. Moreover, the U.S. correlations are very similar to the German:

- Across the sixteen German states, the correlation between the immigrant noncitizen population and *anti*-immigrant attitudes was –0.61 (indicating a moderately negative relationship).
- Across the fifty U.S. states, the correlation between

the immigrant noncitizen population and immigrant-*supportive* attitudes was +0.72.

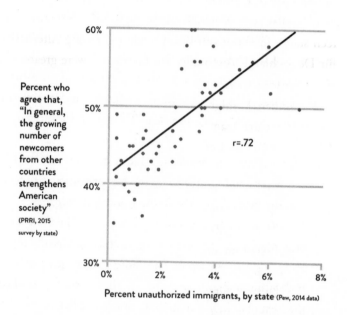

Percent who agree that, "In general, the growing number of newcomers from other countries strengthens American society" (PRRI, 2015 survey by state)

r=.72

Percent unauthorized immigrants, by state (Pew, 2014 data)

The legendary Thomas Pettigrew would not be surprised. Pettigrew, a product of the American South who once was expelled from school for rebutting a bigoted teacher, became a leading prejudice researcher who authored more than five hundred publications and testified in desegregation court cases. In a new article at age eighty-seven (I want to be like him when I grow up), Pettigrew reports on his work with Linda Tropp: in 477 studies of nearly two hundred thousand people across thirty-six cultures, *intergroup contact predicted lower prejudice in every culture.* With cross-racial contact, especially cooperative contact, people develop more favorable racial attitudes. Most such research explores majority-group attitudes toward various minorities (for example, straight people's attitudes toward gay people, not the reverse). And the contact effects are greatest for majority people's attitudes, perhaps because they are less likely to have had contact with those, such as immigrants, who are in a numerical minority.

The contact effect occurs across cultures and domains. In *Social Psychology*, 14th edition, Jean Twenge and I illustrate:

- *South Africa*. The more interracial contact South African Blacks and whites have, the less prejudice they feel, and the more sympathetic their political attitudes.
- *Sexual orientation and transgender identity*. The more contact straight people have with gays and lesbians, the more accepting they become. The more contact people have had with transgender individuals, the less trans prejudice they express. What matters is not just what you know about gay or transgender people but whom you know.
- *Muslims*. The more contact Dutch adolescents have with Muslims, the more accepting of Muslims they are.
- *Roommates and family*. For white students, having a Black roommate improves racial attitudes and leads to greater comfort with those of another race. Other potent connections with a single out-group member, such as an interracial adoption or having a gay child, similarly link people with the out-group and reduce implicit prejudice.
- *Intergenerational*. The more contact younger people

have with older adults, the more favorable their attitudes toward older people.

- *Indirect contact.* Even vicarious indirect contact, via story reading or imagination, or through a friend's having an out-group friend, tends to reduce prejudice. Those who read the Harry Potter books—with their themes of supportive contacts with stigmatized groups—have better attitudes toward immigrants, homosexuals, and refugees. This indirect-contact effect, also called the extended-contact effect, can spread more positive attitudes through a peer group.

So, as white folks get to know Black folks—or as straight folks get to know gay folks, or as citizens get to know immigrants—they become more supportive. The benefit is greatest when contact is friendly and of equal status, and especially when people work cooperatively toward shared goals. But, as we will see, even "mere exposure" to something unfamiliar can increase our liking of it.

In my own midwestern town, where minority students, mostly Hispanic, are a slight majority of public school students, yard signs abound declaring, IMMIGRANTS ARE A BLESSING, NOT A BURDEN. We have known enough immigrants—as neighbors, colleagues, business owners, and workers—to know that today's immigrants, like our own immigrant ancestors, can bless us.

34

IMPLICIT BIAS IS REAL.
CAN TRAINING PROGRAMS
DECREASE IT?

n 2018, a Philadelphia Starbucks manager called the police on two Black men for merely waiting for a friend to arrive. Was this but "an isolated incident"—as 48 percent of white and 10 percent of Black Americans presumed? Or did the arrests reflect "a broader pattern" of bias? Starbucks' CEO later apologized for the incident, said the manager was no longer with the company, and announced that on an upcoming day the company would close eight thousand domestic stores to enable employee racial bias training.

The Starbucks fiasco drew national attention to implicit bias. It also illustrated what we social psychologists overwhelmingly *agree* on, what we *disagree* about, and what can be usefully done.

Agreement: Bias exists, and experiments confirm its pervasiveness. After Amadou Diallo was shot forty-one times by

New York City police after pulling out his wallet, researchers found that non-Black people more often perceived an ambiguous object as a gun when it was held by a Black person. Outside the laboratory, one study sent out five thousand résumés in response to thirteen hundred job ads; applicants with names such as Lakisha and Jamal received one callback for every fifteen sent, while names such as Emily and Greg received one callback for every ten sent. As if aware of the result, Barack Obama reminded Americans to guard "against the subtle impulse to call Johnny back for a job interview but not Jamal." Similar racial disparities have been found in Airbnb inquiry responses, Uber and Lyft pickup requests, and driver treatment during police traffic stops. In one study, Airbnb applicants with seeming African American names "were 16 percent less likely to be accepted relative to identical guests with distinctively white names."

Agreement: Implicit biases underlie many racial disparities. Such biases are modestly revealed by the famed Implicit Association Test (IAT), which assesses how speedily we make associations—a "hammer" with a "nail" rather than a "pail," or a trait with someone of a given race. Across 217 studies, implicit reactions have at least modestly predicted everyday behaviors such as friendliness and discrimination. Likely, the Starbucks manager never consciously thought, "Those two men are Black rather than white, so I'll call the police."

Disagreement: How effective is the IAT at predicting everyday behavior? Its creators remind us that it enables study of a real phenomenon, but was never intended to assess and compare individuals and predict their discrete behaviors. It's much like diet as a risk predictor for heart disease, but not a basis for diagnosing heart disease in an individual.

Disagreement: How effective is implicit bias training? Skeptics argue that "blame and shame" diversity training can backfire, triggering anger and resistance. Or it may seem to normalize bias ("Everybody is biased"). Or it may lead to a temporary improvement in questionnaire responses, but without any lasting benefits. Even the social psychologists Anthony Greenwald and Brian Nosek, two of the IAT co-creators, echo some of these concerns. Greenwald notes that "implicit bias training . . . has not been shown to be effective, and it can even be counterproductive." And Nosek warns that "diversity trainings are filled with good intentions and poor evidence."

But some research offers hope. As part of their research on automatic prejudice, Patricia Devine and her colleagues trained willing volunteers to replace biased with unbiased knee-jerk responses. After explaining and demonstrating the power of implicit biases, Devine and her team taught people strategies for recognizing their own reactions and controlling their automatic responses. People were, for example, trained to imagine examples of people who counter stereotypes, to view others as individuals, to adopt the others' perspective, and to increase their contact with stereotyped people. Throughout the study's follow-up period, participants in their experimental intervention condition displayed reduced implicit prejudice.

Another team of twenty-four researchers held a "research contest" that compared seventeen interventions for reducing unintended prejudice among more than seventeen thousand individuals. Eight of the interventions proved effective, such as by providing vivid, positive examples of Black people who countered stereotypes.

Nosek and Devine collaborated with Patrick Forscher and others on a meta-analysis, a statistical summary, of 494 efforts to change implicit bias. Their conclusion meets in the middle: "implicit bias can be changed, but the effects are often weak" and may not carry over to later behavior.

So, what should we do? And what can we—and Starbucks and other organizations—do to counteract implicit bias?

First, let's not allow our distress to descend to hopeless despair. Reacting with knee-jerk feelings is not unusual; it's what we *do* with that awareness that matters. Do we let those feelings hijack our behavior? Or do we learn to monitor and correct our behavior in future situations? Neuroscience evidence shows that for people who intend no prejudice, the brain can inhibit a momentary flash of unconscious bias in but half a second.

Second, we can aim toward an inclusive multiculturalism. As the race expert Charles Green explains, "Working for racial justice in your organization is not about 'going after' those in the majority. It's about addressing unequal power distribution and creating opportunity for all. It is structural, not personal." Many white people, Green notes, worry that "promoting inclusion is really aimed at unmasking White people as racist" or that "White people will have to lose in order for people of color to win." An inclusive multiculturalism that instead recruits white people as allies can alleviate anxiety and resistance and provide positive energy.

Third, we can articulate clear policies—*behavior* norms—for how people (all people) should be treated in specific situations. Organizations can train employees to enact expected behaviors in various scenarios—how to deal with customers in a coffee shop, with drivers at a traffic stop, with reservation inquiries at a rental unit. Happily, as people *act* without discrimination, they come to *think* with less prejudice. Attitudes follow behavior.

35

HOW POLITICS CHANGES
POLITICIANS

P eople wonder: What explains the political U-turns of so many Republican leaders in their public estimates of Donald Trump? How did Ted Cruz's 2016 assessment ("a pathological liar," "utterly amoral," "a narcissist at a level I don't think this country's ever seen") mutate into his 2020 adulation? How did Lindsey Graham's condemnation (a "race-baiting, xenophobic religious bigot") and Marco Rubio's aspersions ("vulgar," "an embarrassment," "a con artist") metamorphose into both men's ardent defense of Trump?

Republican politics aside, how is it that politicians of any persuasion can so readily morph from disdain to devotion? To defending what they had previously damned? Does such chameleonlike change aim only to please their public? Or does it also reveal an inner change of heart?

Surely the pundits are right to argue that much of this behavior is self-serving—caving in to political pressure, or calculated to cater to shifts in voter opinion. Thus, Carl Bernstein could name twenty-one mostly compliant Republican senators who, in private, "express extreme contempt for Trump and his fitness for office."

Moreover, the phenomenon is bipartisan. The U.S. House once overwhelmingly passed a salary increase for itself in an off-the-record vote, then moments later overwhelmingly defeated the same bill on a public roll-call vote. After 9/11, legislators supported the Iraq war in a three-to-one margin despite many private reservations. And no more do we hear Vice President Kamala Harris declaring, as candidate Harris previously did, that she and Joe Biden would have been on "opposite sides" of school busing.

So yes, public behaviors need not mirror private attitudes. Sometimes we say what we think others want to hear. We are quicker to tell people good news than bad, and we often adjust our message toward our listeners' views.

But there's a second and more psychologically interesting explanation. As social psychological research has repeatedly shown, saying often becomes believing. Attitudes follow behavior.

In experiments, people have been observed to adapt what they say to please their listeners and then to begin believing what they have said. The retired University of Oregon psychologist Ray Hyman experienced the phenomenon: "I started reading palms when I was in my teens as a way to supplement my income from doing magic and mental shows. When I started I did not believe in palmistry. But I knew that to 'sell' it I had to act as if I did. After a few years I became a firm believer in palmistry."

The self-persuasive power of our own public behavior typically happens in small steps. In the Yale social psychologist Stanley Milgram's famous obedience experiments, people began by administering not 450 supposed volts of torture but rather a mild and hardly noticed 15 volts. By the time they followed orders to administer 75 volts to the "learner" and heard the first groan, they had already complied five times, and justified doing so to themselves, after which the next request was for just slightly more. In such a step-by-step fashion, decent people can evolve into agents of cruelty.

Likewise, social movements, from yesterday's Nazism to today's white nationalism, start small and build. More than a hundred "foot in the door" experiments have found that people who have first agreed to a small request later become more likely to comply with a larger request. An initial compliance—signing a petition, wearing a lapel pin, writing an essay, stating one's intention—begins a process that leads people to believe more strongly in what they have said or done. As the social psychologist Robert Cialdini observed in his book *Influence*, "You can use small commitments to manipulate a person's self-image; you can use them to turn citizens into 'public servants,' prospects into 'customers,' prisoners into 'collaborators.'"

Ralph Waldo Emerson anticipated today's social psychology. People's actions "are too strong for them," he noted. They act and then become "the victim and slave" of their action: "What they have done commits and enforces them to do the same again." After inducing Richard Rich to betray Thomas More in *A Man for All Seasons*, Cromwell consoles him: "You'll find it easier next time." Conscience adjusts.

And so it surely has happened among some of the 126 U.S. House members who signed their support of the Texas effort to overturn the presidential election results in Pennsylvania, Georgia, Michigan, and Wisconsin. These onetime Constitution-loving patriots might have strategically hoped to retain the support of their base, preclude a future partisan primary, or avoid the president's scorn. Yet each time one caves, one's morality mutates.

In a 1944 lecture, "The Inner Ring," C. S. Lewis described this slow-cooked process by which the lust for approval and power corrupts. As J. R. R. Tolkien's friend, Lewis was familiar with the draw of the magic ring of power, and not just in the hobbit world.

> Over a drink, or a cup of coffee, disguised as a triviality and sandwiched between two jokes, from the lips of a man, or woman, whom you have recently been getting to know rather better and whom you hope to know better still—just at the moment when you are most anxious not to appear crude, or naïf or a prig—the hint will come. It will be the hint of something which is not quite in accordance with the technical rules of fair play . . . but something, says your new friend, which "we"—and at the word "we" you try not to blush for mere pleasure—something "we always do."
>
> And you will be drawn in . . . because at that moment, when the cup was so near your lips, you cannot bear to be thrust back again into the cold outer world. It would be so terrible to see the other man's face—that

genial, confidential, delightfully sophisticated face—
turn suddenly cold and contemptuous, to know that
you had been tried for the Inner Ring and rejected.
And then, if you are drawn in, next week it will be
something a little further from the rules, and next year
something further still, but all in the jolliest, friendli-
est spirit. It may end in a crash, a scandal, and penal
servitude; it may end in millions, a peerage and giving
prizes at your old school. But you will be a scoundrel.

36

THE POWER OF CONFIRMATION BIAS AND THE CREDIBILITY OF BELIEF

The conservative *New York Times* columnist Ross Douthat spoke for many in being astounded by "the sheer scale of the belief among conservatives that the [2020 presidential] election was really stolen," which he attributed partly to "a strong belief [spurring] people to go out in search of evidence" for what they suppose.

Douthat alluded to *confirmation bias*—our well-established tendency, when assessing our beliefs, to seek information that supports rather than challenges them.

What's the basis for this big idea, which has become one of social psychology's gifts to public awareness? And should appreciating its power to sustain false beliefs cause us to doubt our own core beliefs?

In a pioneering study that explored our greater eagerness to seek evidence *for* rather than *against* our ideas, the psychologist Peter Wason gave British university students a set of three numbers (2, 4, 6) and told them that the series illustrated a rule. Their task was to discover the rule by generating their own three-number sequences, which Wason would confirm either did or didn't conform to the rule. After the students tested enough to feel *certain* they had the rule, they were to announce it.

Imagine being one of Wason's study participants. What might you suppose the rule to be, and what number strings might you offer to test it?

The outcome? Most participants, though seldom right, were never in doubt. Typically, they would form a wrong idea (such as "counting by twos?") and then test it by searching for confirming evidence: "4, 6, 8?" "Yes, that conforms." "20, 22, 24?" "Yes." "200, 202, 204?" "Yes again." "Got it. It's counting by twos." To discover Wason's actual rule (any three ascending numbers), the participants should also have attempted to *disconfirm* their hunch by testing a string that *wasn't* counting by twos.

Confirmation bias also affects our social beliefs. In several experiments, the researchers Mark Snyder and William Swann tasked participants with posing questions to someone that would reveal whether that person was extraverted. The participants' typical strategy was to seek information that would *confirm* extraversion. They would more likely ask "What would you do if you wanted to liven things up at a party?" than "What factors make it hard for you to really open up to people?" Vice versa for those assessing introversion. Thus, participants would typically detect in a person whatever trait they were assessing. Seek and ye shall find.

In everyday life, too, once having formed a belief—that vaccines cause autism, that people can choose or change their sexual orientation, that the election was rigged—we prefer and seek information that verifies our belief.

The phenomenon is politically bipartisan. Across various issues, both conservatives and liberals avoid learning the other side's arguments about topics such as climate change, guns, and same-sex marriage. If we believe that systemic racism is, or is not, rampant, we will gravitate toward news sources, Facebook friends, and evidence that confirm our view, and away from sources that do not. Robert Browning understood: "As is your sort of mind, / So is your sort of search: you'll find / What you desire."

Confirmation bias supplements another idea from social psychology—*belief perseverance*, a sister sort of motivated reasoning. In one provocative experiment, a Stanford research team led by Craig Anderson invited students to consider whether risk takers make good or bad firefighters. Half viewed cases of a venturesome person succeeding as a firefighter, and a cautious person not succeeding; the other half viewed the reverse. After the students formed their conclusion, the researchers asked them to *explain* it. "Of course," one group reflected, "risk takers are braver." To the other group, the opposite explanation seemed equally obvious: "Cautious people have fewer accidents."

When informed that the cases they'd viewed were fake

news made up for the experiment, did the students now return to their pre-experiment neutrality? *No*—because after the fake information was discredited, the students were left with their self-generated explanations of why their initial conclusion *might* be true. Their new beliefs, having grown supporting legs, thus survived the discrediting. As the researchers concluded, "People often cling to their beliefs to a considerably greater extent than is logically or normatively warranted."

So, does confirmation bias plus belief perseverance preclude teaching an old dogma new tricks? Does pondering our beliefs, and considering why they might be true, close us to dissonant truths? Mindful of the self-confirming persistence of our beliefs (whether true or false), should we therefore doubt everything?

Once formed, it does take more compelling persuasion to change a belief ("election fraud was rampant") than it did to create it. But there are at least two reasons we need not succumb to a nihilistic belief in nothing.

1. Evidence-based critical thinking works. Some evidence *will* change our thinking. If I believe that Reno is east of Los Angeles, that Atlanta is east of Detroit, and that Rome is south of New York, a look at a globe will persuade me that I am wrong. I might once have supposed that child-rearing techniques shape children's personalities, that the crime rate has been rising for years, or that traumatic experiences get repressed, but evidence has shown me otherwise. Recognizing that none of us are infallible, we all, thankfully, have at least some amount of intellectual humility.

Moreover, seeking evidence that might disconfirm our convictions sometimes *strengthens* them. I once believed that close, supportive relationships predict happiness, that aerobic exercise boosts mental health, and that wisdom and emotional stability grow with age, and the evidence now enables me to believe these things with even greater confidence. Curiosity is not the enemy of conviction.

2. Explaining a belief does not explain it away. Knowing *why* you believe something needn't tell us anything about your belief's truth or falsity. Consider: if the psychology of belief causes us to question our own beliefs, it can also cause others to question their opposing beliefs, which are themselves prone to confirmation bias and belief perseverance. Psychological science, for example, offers both a psychology of religion and a "psychology of unbelief" (an actual book title). If both fully complete their work—by successfully explaining both religion and irreligion—that leaves open the question of whether theism or atheism is true.

Archbishop William Temple recognized the distinction between explaining a belief and explaining it away when he was reportedly challenged by a student: "Well, of course, Archbishop, the point is that you believe what you believe because of the way you were brought up." To which the archbishop replied, "That is as it may be. But the fact remains that you believe that I believe what I believe because of the way I was brought up, because of the way you were brought up."

Finally, let's remember: if we are left with uncertainty after welcoming both confirming and disconfirming evidence, we can still venture a commitment. As the French author Albert

Camus reportedly observed, sometimes life beckons us to make a 100 percent commitment to something about which we are 51 percent sure—to a cause worth embracing, or even to a belief system that helps make sense of the universe, gives meaning to life, connects us in supportive communities, provides a mandate for morality and selflessness, and offers hope in the face of adversity and death.

So yes, belief perseverance solidifies newly formed ideas as invented rationales outlast the evidence that inspired them. And confirmation bias then sustains our beliefs as we seek belief-confirming evidence. Nevertheless, evidence-based thinking can *strengthen* true beliefs, or at least give us courage, amid lingering doubt, to make a reasoned leap of faith. As Saint Paul advised, "Test everything; hold fast to what is good."

37

FRIENDS VERSUS PHONES

S ome years ago, an NBC *Dateline* producer invited me to her office to brainstorm possible psychology-related segments. But a focused conversation proved difficult, because every three minutes or so she would turn away to check an incoming email or take a call, leaving me feeling a bit demeaned.

In today's smartphone age, such interruptions are pervasive. In the midst of conversation, your friend's attention is diverted by the ding of an incoming message, the buzz of a phone call, or just the urge to check email. You're being *phubbed*—meaning *phone snubbed*.

In one small survey of 143 U.S. adults, 46 percent reported experiencing this with their partners, and 23 percent said it was a problem in their relationship, as when partners glance at their phone during conversation or check it during conversational lulls. "Phubbing" (an Australian-origin term) predicts lower relationship satisfaction. That result would not surprise the evolutionary psychologist David Sbarra and his colleagues, who note "an evolutionary mismatch" between close relationships and smartphones, which "usurp attentional resources" typically allocated to mutual responsiveness.

Could such effects be shown experimentally? A study by Ryan Dwyer and his University of British Columbia colleagues recruited people to share a restaurant meal with their phones on the table or not. "When phones were present (vs. absent), participants felt more distracted, which reduced how much they enjoyed spending time with their friends/family."

Another experiment, by the University of Kent psychologists Varoth Chotpitayasunondh and Karen Douglas, helps explain phone snubbing's social harm. They invited students to put themselves in the skin of a person seen from the back while viewing a three-minute animated conversation. In one condition, the conversational partner sits down, puts the phone on the table, and thereafter never touches it. In a partial phubbing condition, the participant, after thirty seconds, occasionally gazes down at and swipes the phone. In an extensive phubbing condition, the distraction commences immediately and continues. The result: the more phubbing, the more students felt a diminished sense of belonging and self-esteem. Phubbing is micro-ostracism. It leaves someone, even while with another, suddenly alone.

Chotpitayasunondh and Douglas also have found that phubbing can produce a vicious, self-reinforcing cycle "that makes the behavior become normative." Other research reveals that phubbing often provokes resentment, deflated mood, and jealousy. The phone's mere presence decreases people's feelings of closeness with their conversational partner.

Smartphones, to be sure, are a boon to relationships as well as a bane. They connect us to people we don't see, enlarging our sense of belonging. As one who lives thousands of miles from family members, I love FaceTime and messaging. Yet a real touch beats being pinged. A real smile beats an emoticon. An eye-to-eye talk beats an online chat. We are made for face-to-face relationship. Alexander Graham Bell's first-ever phone call was, ironically, a plea for face-to-face contact: "Mr. Watson, come here. I want to see you."

When I mentioned this essay to my wife, Carol, she wryly observed that I (blush) phub her "all the time." So, what can we do, while enjoying our smartphones, to cut the phone snubbing? I reached out to some friends and family and got variations on these ideas:

- "When we get together to play cards, I often put everyone's phone in the next room."
- "When out to dinner, I often ask friends to put their phones away. I find the presence of phones so distracting; the mere threat of interruption diminishes the conversation." Even better: "When some of us go out to dinner, we pile up our phones; the first person to give in and reach for a phone pays for the meal."
- "I sometimes stop talking until the person reestablishes eye contact."
- "I say, 'I hope everything is okay.'" Or this: "I stop and ask, is everything okay? Do you need a minute? I often receive an apology and the phone is put away."
- "I have ADHD and I am easily distracted. Thus, when someone looks at their phone, and I'm distracted, I say,

'I'm sorry, but I am easily distracted. Where was I?' . . . It's extremely effective, because nobody wants me to have to start over."

Seeing phubbing's effects has helped me change my own behavior. Since that unfocused conversation at NBC, I have made a practice, when meeting with someone in my office, to ignore the ringing phone. Nearly always, people pause the conversation to let me take the call. But no, I explain, we are having a conversation and you have taken the time to be here with me. Whoever that is can leave a message or call back. Right now, *you* are who's important.

Come to think of it, I should take that same attitude home.

38

WEALTH, WELL-BEING, AND GENEROSITY

Money matters. For entering U.S. collegians, the number one life goal—surpassing "helping others in difficulty," "raising a family," and seventeen other aspirations—is "being very well off financially." In the most recent UCLA "American Freshman" survey, 82 percent rated being very well-off as "essential" or "very important." Think of it as today's American dream: life, liberty, and the purchase of happiness.

For human flourishing, fiscal fitness indeed matters . . . up to a point. In repeated surveys across nations, a middle-class income—and being able to control one's life—beat being poor. Moreover, people in developed nations tend to be happier and more satisfied than those in the poorest of nations.

But beyond the middle-class level we seem to have an income "satiation point," at which the income–happiness correlation tapers off and happiness no longer increases. For individuals in poor countries, that point is close to $40,000;

for those in rich countries, about $90,000, reports an analysis of 1.7 million Gallup interviews by Andrew Jebb and colleagues.

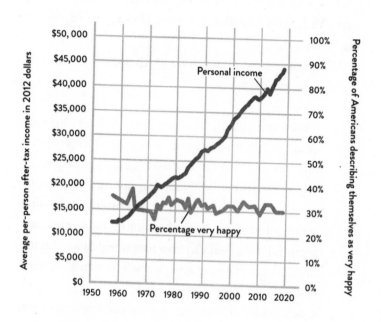

And consider: the average U.S. person's disposable income, adjusted for inflation, has happily tripled over the last sixty years. To be sure, the *average* income increase is partly attributed to greatly increased high incomes. In many countries, including the United States, China, and India, working-class wage earners have experienced a much smaller increase. Simply said, the rising economic tide has lifted the yachts faster than the dinghies.

Even so, few of us wish to return to yesteryear. Most

Americans enjoy today's wonderments, from home air-conditioning to wintertime fresh fruits to smartphones. Yet it's a startling fact: psychological well-being has not floated upward with the rising economic tide. The number of "very happy" adults has remained at three in ten, and depression has been on the rise.

What triggers the diminishing psychological payoff from excess income? Two factors:

1. *Our human capacity for adaptation.* You have surely noticed: we adjust our neutral levels—at which temperatures seem neither hot nor cold, lights neither dim nor bright, events neither gratifying nor disappointing—based on our recent experience. The first chilly day after summer feels colder than the same midwinter temperature. Likewise, wake up to a new world of no bills, no ills, and ample luxury and you will be elated . . . for a while. Continual pleasures subside.

2. *Our tendency to assess our own circumstances by "social comparison" with those around us—and more often those above us.* People with a $40,000 income tend to think $80,000 would enable them to feel wealthy, whereas those at $80,000 say they would need substantially more. Become a millionaire and move to a rich neighborhood, you still may not feel rich. Recall Theodore Roosevelt: "Comparison is the thief of joy."

The outer limit of the relationship between wealth and well-being also appears in two surveys (by Grant Donnelly,

Tianyi Zheng, Emily Haisley, and Michael Norton) of an international bank's high-net-worth clients. Psychologically speaking—as assessed by self-reported life satisfaction and happiness—$2 million and $10 million are about the same.

In some large countries, the economic growth has been accompanied by increasing inequality. And extreme inequality is toxic. In nations or states with greater inequality, lower-income people suffer more ill health, social pathologies, and mental disorders. The same is true of historic times with greater inequality. Show social scientists a time or place with great inequality, and they will likely show you a time or place with a perceived unfairness and mistrust and a high rate of misery, violent crime, obesity, teen births, and more. Disparity dispirits.

People get this. Regardless of politics, most people say they would prefer smaller rich–poor pay gaps. Moreover, those most materialistic—who focus most on gaining wealth—have, ironically, tended to experience lower well-being, especially when seeking wealth to prove themselves or gain power. Those who instead prioritize intimacy, personal growth, and community contribution enjoy a higher life quality.

If wealth increases well-being only up to a point—and much evidence indicates that is so—and if extreme inequality is socially toxic, then could societies increase human flourishing with economic and tax policies that spread wealth?

Let's make this personal: If earning, accumulating, and spending money increase our happiness only to a satiation point, then why do we spend our money for (quoting the prophet Isaiah) "that which is not bread" and our "labor for that which does not satisfy"? Quite apart from moral considerations, what's to be lost by sharing our wealth above the income–happiness satiation point?

39

THE MERE EXPOSURE EFFECT: FAMILIARITY BREEDS CONTENT

Hidden beneath most unconscious prejudice is a simple natural bias—a preference for what's familiar and a wariness of things unfamiliar. This seemingly hardwired tendency led our ancestors to respond adaptively to things that were either familiar and generally safe or unfamiliar and possibly dangerous. "If it's familiar," the researcher Robert Zajonc once said, "it has not eaten you yet."

Although this principle may strike you as unremarkable, you may find the range of the evidence more surprising.

The basic finding: familiarity fosters fondness. Familiarity affects our reactions to people. As two strangers continue interacting, they begin to find each other more attractive. Physical imperfections become less noticed. As we become familiar with others, we usually begin to like them more and perceive them as more trustworthy. Adults who have knowingly known LGBTQ folks eventually become more supportive of them. Even infants, by three months, begin to prefer photos of the race they see most often—usually, of course, their own race.

This *mere exposure effect*, replicated in study after study, was belatedly recognized by the young Taiwanese man who sent more than seven hundred letters to his girlfriend, including an invitation to marry him. In the end, she did marry—the mail carrier.

The phenomenon also occurs as people repeatedly experience novel nonsense syllables, musical selections, geometric figures, paintings, faces, or even Chinese ideographs.

For example, make a guess: Do the made-up "Turkish" words *nansoma*, *afworbu*, and *ikitaf* mean something better or worse than *saricik*, *ikadirga*, and *biwojni*? When Zajonc showed University of Michigan students these nonsense words a varying number of times, they tended to rate more positively those they had seen most frequently. (My students, too, by the semester's end, have liked best those meaningless nonsense words that I periodically flashed at them.)

The mere exposure effect runs counter to our expectation that exposure produces boredom—or worse, that familiarity breeds contempt. As children and adults repeatedly sample unfamiliar foods or music, they typically come to like them better—though only to a point. If repetitions are incessant, our increasing liking of a popular song may reverse. With unremitting repetition comes satiation.

Even more unexpectedly, the familiarity-feeds-fondness phenomenon even occurs when people experience a stimulus *without their awareness*. When people hear music in one earpiece while focusing on repeated words spoken into the other earpiece, they will later prefer the previously heard tunes—*even though they do not recognize them* among other tunes not previously experienced. Likewise, amnesia patients who do not recall their experiences will still prefer recently seen faces.

These experiments illustrate another basic fact of our human nature: our emotions are often separate from our thinking. "Affect may precede cognition," surmised Zajonc. This occurs because emotions and thinking are processed by different brain areas.

To appreciate the mere exposure effect in action, consider these examples.

Art appreciation. When Grand Rapids, Michigan's giant Calder sculpture was installed on its city hall plaza, people rolled their eyes. "If you took a Calder and put it next to a pile of welded junk and didn't tell the average person which was which, 99 out of 100 people wouldn't know the difference," said one critic. Today, it is the city's beloved symbol.

And do we really adore the *Mona Lisa*'s inherent artistry when visiting the Louvre, or are we just delighted to find a familiar face? Perhaps both. When the researchers Eddie Harmon-Jones and John Allen repeatedly showed people a woman's face, their viewers' smiling muscles became more active with repeated viewings.

Liking advertised products. Persuaders understand these principles. After repetitions of an ad, shoppers may have an automatic inclination to prefer the familiar product. Even when not remembering the ad, they may reach for the advertised product.

Liking our familiar selves. We also like best our own

familiar face. When shown a picture of themselves and a picture of their mirror image, which do you suppose people prefer?

In an experiment, they preferred their most familiar image—the one they saw daily in a mirror. (Perhaps you've noticed that photos of you never look quite right?) When the participants' close friends were shown the same two pictures, they preferred the photo that showed the face with which they were familiar.

Liking familiar candidates. When candidates are well known, political ads matter little. When candidates are unknown, media exposure often predicts winners. When running for drain commissioner, the candidate with the familiar name may get your vote.

In 1990, the admired Washington State Supreme Court chief, Keith Callow, came to understand this. He lost his re-election bid to an unknown attorney, Charles Johnson, who filed for the election because he believed that judges "need to be challenged." With the outcome a foregone conclusion (of course Callow would win!), neither campaigned and the media ignored the race. When voters were given the two candidate names on Election Day with no further identification, the result was a stunning 53 percent to 47 percent Johnson victory. As the ousted judge conjectured to the incredulous legal community, "There are a lot more Johnsons out there than Callows." Indeed, there were twenty-seven "Charles Johnsons" in just the Seattle phone book. Forced to choose between two unknowns, people preferred the familiar, likable-seeming name of Charles Johnson.

Our preference for the familiar is akin to, and likely feeds, the persuasive power of repetition. As mere exposure breeds liking, so mere repetition breeds belief. Repeated statements— "The Cadillac Seville has the best repair record"—become easy to process and remember, and thus to seem more true.

Social psychologists have found such findings "scary." The mere repetition effect is well understood by political manipulators. Easy-to-remember lies can overwhelm hard truths. "Vaccines cause autism." "Climate change is a hoax." "Crooked Hillary."

George Orwell understood. His world of *Nineteen Eighty-Four* harnessed the controlling power of mere repetition. "Freedom is slavery." "Ignorance is strength." "War is peace." As Hitler explained in *Mein Kampf*, "All effective propaganda must be limited to a very few points and must harp on these in slogans." Familiarity breeds belief.

40

DO REPLICATION FAILURES DISCREDIT PSYCHOLOGICAL SCIENCE?

P sychological science has taken some body blows of late, with famous findings challenged by seeming failures to replicate them.

The problem isn't just that some prolific researchers faked data and that the famed psychologists David Rosenhan and Hans Eysenck have been accused of doing likewise. Every discipline has a few self-promoting deceivers, and more who bend the truth to their side.

And it's not just critics arguing that a few celebrated findings, such as the tribalism of the renowned Stanford Prison and Robbers Cave experiments, were supposedly one-off, stage-managed happenings. Or that some findings of enormous popular interest—brain training for older folks, implicit bias training programs, or teaching to learning styles—all produce little enduring benefit.

The problem is that certain other findings have not been consistently reproducible. The effects of teachers' expectations, power posing, willpower depletion, facial feedback (feeling the face you make), and wintertime depression (seasonal affective disorder) have often failed to replicate or now seem more modest than widely claimed.

Moreover, the magnitude and reliability of stereotype threat, growth mindset benefits, and the marshmallow test (showing the life success of four-year-olds who can delay gratification) are, say skeptics, more mixed and variable—more modest—than often presumed.

Hoo, boy. What's left? Does psychology's knowledge storehouse have empty shelves? Are students and the public justifiably dismayed? As one former psychology student tweeted, "I took a [high school] psychology class whose entire content was all of these famous experiments that have turned out to be total horseshit. I studied this! They made me take an exam! For what?" To which others responded,

- "I'm putting all my chips on neuroscience, I refuse to listen to psychologists ever again, they had their chance."
- "Imagine if you'd spent 10 years getting a PhD in this stuff, going into $200k in debt."
- "You can learn more from life never mind a psychology lesson just take a look around fella."
- "I have a whole damn degree full of this @#$%."

But consider:

1. *How science works.* Yes, some widely publicized studies haven't replicated well. In response to this, we text-book authors adjust our reporting. In contrast to simple common sense and to conspiracy theories, science is a self-checking, self-correcting process that gradually weeds out oversimplifications and falsehoods. As with mountain climbing, the upward march of science comes with occasional down slopes.

2. *Some phenomena are genuine, but situation specific.* Some of the disputed phenomena actually have been replicated, under known conditions. One of my favorite but contested experiments—the happy pen-in-the-lips versus pouting pen-in-the-teeth facial feedback effect—turns out to replicate best when people are not distracted by being videotaped (as happened in the failure-to-replicate experiments). And stepping back to look at the bigger picture, the Center for Open Science reports that its forthcoming analysis of 307 psychological science replications found that 64 percent obtained statistically significant results in the same direction as original studies, with effect sizes averaging 68 percent as large. The bottom line: many phenomena *do* replicate.

3. *What endures and is left to teach is . . . everything else.* Memories really are malleable. Expectations really do influence our perceptions. Information really does occur on two tracks—explicit and implicit (and implicit bias is real). Partial reinforcement really does increase resistance to extinction. Human traits really are

influenced by many genes having small effects. Group polarization really does amplify our group differences. In-group bias really is powerful and perilous. An ability to delay gratification really does increase future life success. We really do often fear the wrong things. Sexual orientation really is a natural disposition that's neither willfully chosen nor willfully changed. Split-brain experiments really have revealed complementary functions of our two brain hemispheres. Electroconvulsive therapy really is a shockingly effective treatment for intractable depression. Sleep experiments really have taught us much about our sleeping and dreaming. Blindsight really does indicate our capacity for visual processing without awareness. Frequent quizzing and self-testing really do boost students' retention. But enough. The list of repeatedly confirmed, humanly significant phenomena could go on for pages.

So, *yes*, let's teach the importance of replication for winnowing truth. Let's separate the wheat from the chaff. Let's encourage critical thinking that's seasoned with healthy skepticism but not science-scorning cynicism. And let us also be reassured that our evidence-derived principles of human behavior are overwhelmingly worth teaching as we help our students appreciate their wonder-full world.

NOTES

1. IMPLICIT EGOTISM

3 *Such is the implication of* implicit egotism: Brett W. Pelham, Mauricio Carvallo, and John T. Jones, "Implicit Egotism," *Current Directions in Psychological Science* 14, no. 5 (2005): 106–10, doi.org/10.1111/j.0963-7214.2005.00344.x.

3 *We also find someone more attractive*: Chris R. Fraley and Michael J. Marks, "Westermarck, Freud, and the Incest Taboo: Does Familial Resemblance Activate Sexual Attraction?," *Personality and Social Psychology Bulletin* 36, no. 9 (2010): 1202–12, doi.org/10.1177/0146167210377180; Bruno Laeng, Oddrun Vermeer, and Unni Sulutvedt, "Is Beauty in the Face of the Beholder?," *PLOS One* 8, no. 7 (2013): e68395, doi.org/10.1371/journal.pone.0068395.

4 *People of varied nationalities*: John T. Jones et al., "Name Letter Preferences Are Not Merely Mere Exposure: Implicit Egotism as Self-Regulation," *Journal of Experimental Social Psychology* 38, no. 2 (2002): 170–77, doi.org/10.1006/jesp.2001.1497.

4 *People also tend to marry someone*: John T. Jones et al., "How Do I Love Thee? Let Me Count the Js: Implicit Egotism and Interpersonal Attraction," *Journal of Personality and Social Psychology* 87, no. 5 (2004): 665–83, doi.org/10.1037/0022-3514.87.5.665.

4 *People likewise prefer the numbers*: S. L. Koole, A. Dijksterhuis, and A. Van Knippenberg, "What's in a Name: Implicit Self-Esteem and the

Automatic Self," *Journal of Personality and Social Psychology* 80, no. 4 (2001): 669–85, doi.org/10.1037//0022-3514.80.4.669.

4 *"were more attracted than usual"*: Jones et al., "How Do I Love Thee?"

4 *people seem to gravitate to careers*: Brett W. Pelham and M. C. Mirenberg, "Why Susie Sells Seashells by the Seashore: Implicit Egotism and Major Life Decisions," *Journal of Personality and Social Psychology* 41, no. 4 (2002): 84–89, doi.org/10.1037//0022-3514.82.4.469.

5 *people named Baker, Barber, Butcher*: Brett Pelham, "Why We Love People, Places, and Things That Resemble Us," *Character and Context*, Society for Personality and Social Psychology, May 14, 2019, www.spsp .org/news-center/blog/pelham-things-that-resemble-us.

2. THE AMAZING POWER OF ATTENTION

8 *As the mind-messing magician Teller*: Jonah Lehrer, "Magic and the Brain: Teller Reveals the Neuroscience of Illusion," *Wired*, April 20, 2009, www.wired.com/2009/04/ff-neuroscienceofmagic/.

8 *One Swedish psychologist, after being surprised*: Alberto Gallace, "Living with Touch," *Psychologist* 25, no. 12 (2012): 896–99, thepsychologist .bps.org.uk/volume-25/edition-12/living-touch.

9 *The researchers pipe novel tunes*: William R. Wilson, "Feeling More Than We Can Know: Exposure Effects Without Learning," *Journal of Personality and Social Psychology* 37, no. 6 (1979): 811–21, psycnet.apa.org /buy/1980-29585-001.

9 *In an acoustic replication of the invisible gorilla study*: Polly Dalton and Nick Fraenkel, "Gorillas We Have Missed: Sustained Inattentional Deafness for Dynamic Events," *Cognition* 124, no. 3 (2012): 367–72, doi.org/10.1016/j.cognition.2012.05.012.

10 *Dalton (working with Sandra Murphy)*: Sandra Murphy and Polly Dalton, "Inattentional Numbness and the Influence of Task Difficulty," *Cognition* 178 (2018): 1–6, doi.org/10.1016/j.cognition.2018 .05.001.

10 *Another British experiment, this one by Sophie*: Sophie Forster and Charles Spence, "'What Smell?': Temporarily Loading Visual Attention Reduces a Prolonged Loss of Olfactory Awareness," *Psychological Science* 29, no. 10 (2018): 1642–52, doi.org/10.1177/0956797618781325.

10 *Can we expect a demonstration*: Cleveland Clinic, last reviewed

September 29, 2021, https://my.clevelandclinic.org/health/diseases/21850-ageusia-loss-of-sense-of-taste.

3. THERE IS MORE TO HEARING THAN MEETS THE EARS

12 *So it was when the writer Sylvia Wright*: Sylvia Wright, "The Death of Lady Mondegreen," *Harper's Magazine*, November 1954, harpers.org/archive/1954/11/the-death-of-lady-mondegreen/.

13 *While listening to sad rather than happy music*: Jamin B. Halberstadt, Paula M. Niedenthal, and Julia Kushner, "Resolution of Lexical Ambiguity by Emotional State," *Psychological Science* 6, no. 5 (1995): 278–82, doi.org/10.1111/j.1467-9280.1995.tb00511.x.

4. HOW DO WE KNOW OURSELVES?

17 *We know ourselves partly by observing*: Daryl J. Bem, "Self-Perception Theory," *Advances in Experimental Psychology* 6 (1972): 1–62, doi.org/10.1016/S0065-2601(08)60024-6.

17 *The limits of such self-revelation*: Andreas Lind et al., "Speakers' Acceptance of Real-Time Speech Exchange Indicates That We Use Auditory Feedback to Specify the Meaning of What We Say," *Psychological Science* 25, no. 6 (2013): 1198–205, doi.org/10.1177%2F0956797614529797.

18 *Let Botox paralyze your facial muscles*: Axel M. Wollmer et al., "Facing Depression with Botulinum Toxin: A Randomized Control Trial," *Journal of Psychiatric Research* 46, no. 5 (2012): 574–81, doi.org/10.1016/j.jpsychires.2012.01.027.

18 *silently read nonsense words and names*: David Myers, "How Do We Know Ourselves? If You Said One Thing and Heard Yourself Saying Another, What Would You Think You Said?," Macmillan Learning, September 9, 2014, community.macmillanlearning.com/t5/psychology-blog/how-do-we-know-ourselves-if-you-said-one-thing-and-heard/ba-p/5248?src=college.

19 *Take a walk with short, shuffling steps*: William Flack, "Peripheral Feedback Effects of Facial Expressions, Bodily Postures, and Vocal Expressions on Emotional Feelings," *Cognition and Emotion* 20, no. 2 (2006): 177–95, doi.org/10.1080/02699930500359617.

19 *"test headphone sets" by making*: Gary L. Wells and Richard E. Petty, "The Effect of Overt Head Movements on Persuasion: Compatibility

and Incompatibility of Responses," *Basic and Applied Social Psychology* 1, no. 3 (1980): 219–30, doi.org/10.1207/s15324834basp0103_2.

19 *American psychology students rated neutral stimuli*: John T. Cacioppo, Joseph R. Priester, and Gary Berntson, "Rudimentary Determinants of Attitudes: II. Arm Flexion and Extension Have Differential Effects on Attitudes," *Journal of Personality and Social Psychology* 65 (1993): 5–17, doi.org/10.1037/0022-3514.65.1.5.

5. DUAL PROCESSING: ONE BRAIN, TWO MINDS?

24 *magnetic stimulation to deactivate people's sense of touch*: Tony Ro and Lua Koenig, "Unconscious Touch Perception After Disruption of the Primary Somatosensory Cortex," *Psychological Science* 32, no. 4 (2021): 549–57, doi.org/10.1177/0956797620970551.

24 *brain-damaged patient whose amnesia*: Joseph LeDoux, *The Emotional Brain: The Mysterious Underpinnings of Emotional Life* (New York: Simon & Schuster, 1996).

25 *"I've known H.M. since 1962"*: Suzanne Corkin, quoted by R. Adelson, "Lessons from H.M.," *Monitor on Psychology* 36, no. 8 (2005): 59, www.apa.org/monitor/sep05/lessons.

25 *Jimmie, who, after a 1945 brain injury*: Oliver Sacks, *The Man Who Mistook His Wife for a Hat* (London: Duckworth Books, 1985).

26 *"80 to 90 percent of what we do"*: Kandel, interview by Steve Ayan, "Speaking of Memory," *Scientific American Mind*, October/November 2008, wtri.com/wp-content/uploads/2015/06/Speaking-of-Memory.pdf.

6. MAKING NEW YEAR'S RESOLUTIONS THAT LAST

28 *challenging goals motivate achievement*: Gary P. Latham and Edwin A. Locke, "New Developments in and Directions for Goal-Setting Research," *European Psychologist* 12, no. 4 (2007): 290–300, doi.org/10.1027/1016-9040.12.4.290.

28 *Research shows that people who flesh out goals*: P. M. Gollwitzer and G. Oettingen, "Implementation Intentions," in *Encyclopedia of Behavioral Medicine*, ed. Marc D. Gellman and J. Rick Turner (New York: Springer, 2013), 1043–48.

28 *when that progress is displayed publicly*: Benjamin Harkin et al., "Does

Monitoring Goal Progress Promote Goal Attainment? A Meta-analysis of the Experimental Evidence," *Psychology Bulletin* 142, no. 2 (2016): 198–229, doi.org/10.1037/bul0000025.

28 *Such "situational self-control strategies"*: Angela L. Duckworth, Tamar Szabo Gendler, and James J. Gross, "Situational Strategies for Self-Control," *Perspectives on Psychological Science* 11, no. 1 (2016): 35–55, doi.org/10.1177/1745691615623247.

29 *the key is forming beneficial habits*: Brian M. Gala and Angela L. Duckworth, "More Than Resisting Temptation: Beneficial Habits Mediate the Relationship Between Self-Control and Positive Life Outcomes," *Journal of Personality and Social Psychology* 109, no. 3 (2015): 508–25, doi.org/10.1037/pspp0000026.

29 *"If you would make anything a habit"*: From *The Discourses of Epictetus*, www.gutenberg.org/files/10661/10661-h/10661-h.htm.

29 *Jane Coaston explained*: "Don't Tell Me You Already Gave Up on Your Resolutions!," *New York Times*, January 8, 2022.

29 *Phillippa Lally asked ninety-six university students*: Phillippa Lally et al., "How Are Habits Formed: Modelling Habit Formation in the Real World," *European Journal of Social Psychology* 40, no. 6 (2010): 998–1009, doi.org/10.1002/ejsp.674.

30 *"You'll see I wear only gray or blue suits"*: Michael Lewis, "Obama's Way," *Vanity Fair*, October 2012, www.vanityfair.com/news/2012/10/michael-lewis-profile-barack-obama.

31 *"Civilization advances by extending"*: Alfred North Whitehead, *Introduction to Mathematics* (London: Williams and Norgate, 1911).

7. THE POWERS AND PERILS OF INTUITION

32 *"Buried deep within each"*: Prince Charles, interview by James Naughtie, BBC Online Network (2000), news.bbc.co.uk/hi/english/static/events/reith_2000/lecture6.stm.

32 *"I'm a gut player"*: Bush, interview by Barbara Walters, ABC News, January 6, 2006, abcnews.go.com/2020/story?id=123552&page=1.

32 *"able to get a sense"*: "Slovenia Summit 2001," White House Archives, https://georgewbush-whitehouse.archives.gov/news/releases/2001/06/20010618.html.

33 *"The first principle," said Feynman*: Richard P. Feynman, Speech, Caltech's 1974 Commencement Address, www.quotationspage.com/quote/523 .html.

34 *We are skilled at reading "thin slices"*: Ambady Nalinia and Robert Rosenthal, "Half a Minute: Predicting Teacher Evaluations from Thin Slices of Nonverbal Behavior and Physical Attractiveness," *Journal of Personality and Social Psychology* 64, no. 3 (1993): 431–41, kevin .burke.dev/pdf/30_seconds_teacher_quality.pdf.

34 *"We're finding that everything is evaluated"*: Bargh, quoted by Beth Azar, "Split-Second Evaluations Shape Our Moods, Actions," *Monitor American Psychological Association* 29, no. 9 (1998).

35 *the mate-selection process*: Jason Dana, Robyn Dawes, and Nathaniel Peterson, "Belief in the Unstructured Interview: The Persistence of an Illusion," *Judgment and Decision Making* 8, no. 5 (2013): 512–20, journal.sjdm.org/12/121130a/jdm121130a.pdf.

36 *why aren't stock market day traders*: Burton G. Malkiel, *A Random Walk Down Wall Street: The Time-Tested Strategy for Successful Investing* (New York: W. W. Norton, 1973).

36 *if such psychic intuitions were commonplace*: Michael Shermer, "If That's True, What Else Would Be True?," *Skeptic* 7, no. 4 (1999): 102–103.

8. FEARING THE RIGHT THINGS

37 *In a late 2020 Gallup World Poll*: Jonathan Rothwell, "Fear and Social Distancing: Global Perceptions of Risk Vary," Gallup, December 28, 2020, news.gallup.com/opinion/gallup/328187/fear-social-distancing -global-perceptions-risk-vary.aspx?utm_source=alert&utm_medium =email&utm_content=morelink&utm_campaign=syndication.

37 *a hundredfold lower death risk*: Centers for Disease Control, "Covid-19 Risks and Vaccine Information for Older Adults," August 2, 2021.

39 *Gallup reports that nearly half*: Megan Brenan, "Nearly Half in U.S. Fear Being the Victim of a Mass Shooting," Gallup, September 10, 2019, news.gallup.com/poll/266681/nearly-half-fear-victim-mass-shooting .aspx?utm_source=alert&utm_medium=email&utm_content=morelink &utm_campaign=syndication.

39 *transforming schools into fortresses*: Jillian Peterson, Ellen Sackrison, and Angela Polland, "Training Students to Respond to Shootings on

Campus: Is It Worth It?," *Journal of Threat Assessment and Management* 2, no. 2 (2015): 127–38, doi.org/10.1037/tam0000042.

39 *Guns kill more than forty thousand Americans*: Centers for Disease Control, "All Injuries," last reviewed April 9, 2021, www.cdc.gov/nchs /fastats/injury.htm.

39 *Among the victims are more children*: Meredith Wadman, "Guns Kill More U.S. Kids Than Cancer. This Emergency Physician Aims to Prevent Those Firearm Deaths," *Science*, December 6, 2018, www.science .org/news/2018/12/guns-kill-more-us-kids-cancer-emergency-physician -aims-prevent-those-firearm-deaths.

39 *the likelihood of any given student*: David Ropeik, "School Shootings Are Extraordinarily Rare. Why Is Fear of Them Driving Policy?," *Washington Post*, March 8, 2018, www.washingtonpost.com/outlook/school -shootings-are-extraordinarily-rare-why-is-fear-of-them-driving-policy /2018/03/08/f4ead9f2-2247-11e8-94da-ebf9d112159c_story.html.

39 *a dramatic drop from 1993 to 2019*: Centers for Disease Control, "Youth Risk Behavior Surveillance System," last reviewed October 27, 2020, www.cdc.gov/healthyyouth/data/yrbs/index.htm.

40 *vulnerability to a school shooting*: National Center for Education Statistics, "Educational Institutions," nces.ed.gov/fastfacts/display.asp?id=84.

40 *2,829 teens died in motor vehicle crashes*: David Leonhardt, "Letting Teenagers Live," *New York Times*, March 4, 2018, www.nytimes.com /2018/03/04/opinion/teenagers-driving-cars-guns.html.

40 *"If the Stoneman Douglas shooting"*: Leonhardt, "Letting Teenagers Live."

40 *As an example, he argued for*: Centers for Disease Control, "Graduated Driver License," last reviewed August 19, 2016, www.cdc.gov/phlp /publications/topic/gdl.html.

9. WE KNEW IT ALL ALONG

43 *Proverbs are typically short and memorable*: Karl Halvor Teigen, "Old Truths or Fresh Insights? A Study of Students' Evaluations of Proverbs," *Social Psychology* 25, no. 1 (1986): 43–49, doi.org/10.1111/j .2044-8309.1986.tb00700.x.

44 *The point of the phenomenon*: Neal J. Roese and Kathleen D. Vohs, "Hindsight Bias," *Perspectives on Psychological Science* 7, no. 5 (2012): 411–26, doi.org/10.1177%2F1745691612454303.

45 *A U.S. Senate investigative report*: Malcolm Gladwell, "Connecting the Dots," *New Yorker*, March 2, 2003.

10. JUDGING OTHERS AND JUDGING OURSELVES

47 *"As we pull down controversial statues"*: Nicholas Kristof, "The Mistakes That Will Haunt Our Legacy," *New York Times*, July 11, 2020, www.nytimes.com/2020/07/11/opinion/sunday/animal-rights-cruelty.html.

48 *"what their position on slavery"*: Robert P. George (@McCormickProf), Twitter, July 1, 2020, 11:23 p.m., twitter.com/McCormickProf/status/1278529694355292161.

49 *people do err when confidently predicting*: Janet K. Swim and Lauri L. Hyers, "Excuse Me—What Did You Just Say?! Women's Private and Public Responses to Sexist Remarks," *Journal of Experimental Social Psychology* 35, no. 1 (1999): 68–88, doi.org/10.1006/jesp.1998.1370; Kerry Kawakami, Elizabeth Dunn, and John F. Dovidio, "Mispredicting Affective and Behavioral Responses to Racism," *Science* 323, no. 5911 (2009): 276–78, doi.org/10.1126/science.1164951.

11. BEHAVIORAL CONFIRMATION: GETTING WHAT WE EXPECT

51 *experiment with fifty-one undergraduate pairs*: Mark Snyder, "When Belief Creates Reality," *Advances in Experimental Psychology* 18 (1984): 247–305, doi.org/10.1016/S0065-2601(08)60146-X.

52 *tell one class they should be neat and tidy*: Richard L. Miller, Philip Brickman, and Diana Bolen, "Attribution Versus Persuasion as a Means for Modifying Behavior," *Journal of Personality and Social Psychology* 31, no. 3 (1975): 430–41, psycnet.apa.org/doi/10.1037/h0076539.

52 *Sandra Murray from her studies of dating couples*: Sandra L. Murray, John G. Holmes, and Dale W. Griffin, "The Benefits of Positive Illusions: Idealization and the Construction of Satisfaction in Close Relationships," *Journal of Personality and Psychology* 70, no. 1 (1996): 79–98, psycnet.apa.org/doi/10.1037/0022-3514.70.1.79; Sandra L. Murray, John G. Holmes, and Dale W. Griffin, "The Self-Fulfilling Nature of Positive Illusions in Romantic Relationships: Love Is Not Blind but Prescient," *Journal of Personality and Psychology* 71, no. 6 (1996): 1155–80, doi.org/10.1037//0022-3514.71.6.1155; Sandra L. Murray, John G. Holmes, and Dale W. Griffin, "Self-Esteem and the Quest for Felt Security: How

Perceived Regard Regulates Attachment Processes," *Journal of Personality and Psychology* 78, no. 3 (2000): 478–98, doi.org/10.1037//0022-3514.78.3.478.

12. HOW DO I LOVE ME? LET ME COUNT THE WAYS

54 *Carl Rogers once objected to the religious doctrine*: Reinhold Niebuhr, *The Self and the Dramas of History* (New York: Scribner, 1955).

13. THE SCIENCE OF HUMILITY

65 *"We must always take sides"*: Elie Wiesel, *The Night Trilogy: Night, Dawn, Day* (New York: Hill and Wang, 2008).

65 *the percentage of both Republicans and Democrats*: Marc Hetherington and Jonathan Weiler, *Prius or Pickup? How the Answers to Four Simple Questions Explain America's Great Divide* (Boston: Houghton Mifflin Harcourt, 2018).

66 *"Each nation feels superior to other nations"*: Dale Carnegie, *How to Win Friends and Influence People* (New York: Simon & Schuster, 1937).

66 *Humility, by contrast, entails* an accurate self-understanding: Daryl R. Van Tongeren and David G. Myers, "A Social Psychological Perspective on Humility," in *Handbook of Humility*, ed. Everett L. Worthington Jr., Don E. Davis, and Joshua N. Hook (New York: Routledge, 2016).

67 *their research on the humblebrag*: Ovul Sezer, Francesca Gino, and Michael Norton, "Humblebragging: A Distinct—and Ineffective—Self-Presentation Strategy," *Journal of Personality and Social Psychology* 114, no. 1 (2018): 52–74, doi.org/10.1037/pspi0000108.

67 *good lives and healthy cultures*: Van Tongeren and Myers, "Social Psychological Perspective on Humility."

68 *"The new Pope is a humble man, very much like me"*: Donald Trump (@realDonaldTrump), Twitter, Dec. 25, 2013, twitter.com/realDonaldTrump/status/415868924841189376.

68 *"If anyone would like to acquire"*: C. S. Lewis, *Mere Christianity* (London: Geoffrey Bles, 1952).

14. WHEN BIRTH ORDER MATTERS

71 *No wonder firstborns have been consistently*: Abby Jackson, "Every Year, Firstborn Kids Dominate Harvard's Freshman Class," *Business Insider*,

August 31, 2017, www.businessinsider.com/harvard-freshman-class
-birth-order-2017-8.

71 *later-born people, studies find*: Tomás Lejarraga et al., "No Effect of Birth
Order on Adult Risk Taking," *Proceedings of the National Academy of Sciences* 116, no. 13 (2019): 6019–24, doi.org/10.1073/pnas.1814153116.

71 *firstborn individuals do not differ*: Julia Rohrer, Boris Egloff, and Stefan
C. Schmukle, "Birth Order Effects on Personality," *Proceedings of the
National Academy of Sciences* 112, no. 46 (2015): 14224–29, doi.org
/10.1073/pnas.1506451112; Julia M. Rohrer, Boris Egloff, and Stefan
C. Schmukle, "Probing Birth-Order Effects on Narrow Traits Using
Specification-Curve Analysis," *Psychological Science* 28, no. 12 (2017):
1821–32, doi.org/10.1177%2F0956797617723726; Rodica Ioana
Damian and Brent W. Roberts, "The Associations of Birth Order with
Personality and Intelligence in a Representative Sample of U.S. High
School Students," *Journal of Research in Personality* 58 (2015): 96–105,
doi.org/10.1016/j.jrp.2015.05.005.

72 *as the late Judith Rich Harris argued*: Judith Rich Harris, "Why Do
People Believe That Birth Order Has Important Effects on Personality?," *Judith Rich Harris*, January 17, 2002, judithrichharris.info/tna
/birth-order/believe.htm.

72 *the odds of same-sex attraction*: Ray Blanchard, "Recent Findings on Fraternal Birth Order and Homosexuality in Males," *Archives of Sexual Behavior* 48 (2019): 1899–900, doi.org/10.1007/s10508-019-01504-0;
Anthony F. Bogaert and Malvina N. Skorska, "A Short Review of
Biological Research on the Development of Sexual Orientation,"
Hormones and Behavior 119, no. 10 (2020): 46–59, doi.org/10.1016
/j.yhbeh.2019.104659; J. Michael Bailey et al., "Sexual Orientation,
Controversy, and Science," *Psychological Science in the Public Interest* 17,
no. 2 (2016): 45–101, doi.org/10.1177/1529100616637616.

73 *Bogaert and his colleagues have now confirmed*: Bogaert and Skorska,
"Short Review of Biological Research on the Development of Sexual
Orientation."

15. CARDIAC ARREST AND THE CONSCIOUS EXPERIENCE OF DEATH

75 *blood infusion four hours after death*: Zvonimir Vrselja et al., "Restoration of Brain Circulation and Cellular Functions Hours Post-

mortem," *Nature* 568 (2019): 336–43, doi.org/10.1038/s41586-019
-1099-1.

76 *A* Newsweek *cover showing a resuscitated heart attack*: *Newsweek*, July
23, 2007.

76 *Of 2.8 million CDC-reported deaths*: Sherry L. Murphy et al., "Mortality in the United States, 2017," Centers for Disease Control, November
2018, www.cdc.gov/nchs/products/databriefs/db328.htm.

77 *Parnia offers his multisite study*: Sam Parnia et al., "AWARE—
AWAreness During REsuscitation: A Prospective Study," *Resuscitation*
85, no. 12 (2014): 1799–805, doi.org/10.1016/j.resuscitation.2014
.09.004.

78 *do report a cognitive experience*: Mario Beauregard, Évelyne Landry
St-Pierre, Gabrielle Rayburn, and Philippe Demers, "Conscious Men-
tal Activity During a Deep Hypothermic Cardiocirculatory Arrest?,"
Resuscitation 83 (2012): e19, www.resuscitationjournal.com/article
/S0300-9572(11)00575-2/pdf.

78 *methods with the Open Science Framework*: OSFHome, osf.io.

79 *"It wasn't what I expected"*: Agatha Christie, *The Thirteen Problems* (London: Collins, 1932).

16. DO PEOPLE REPRESS—OR VIVIDLY
REMEMBER—TRAUMATIC EVENTS?

82 *tracked down fifteen of her fellow passengers*: Margaret C. McKinnon,
Daniel J. Palombo, Anthony Nazarov, Namita Kumar, Wayne Khuu,
and Brian Levine, "Threat of Death and Autobiographical Memory: A
Study of Passengers from Flight AT236," *Clinical Psychological Science*
18 (2015): 487–502.

83 *The persistent memories from Flight AT236*: Stephen Porter and Kristine
A. Peace, "The Scars of Memory: A Prospective, Longitudinal Investigation of the Consistency of Traumatic and Positive Emotional Memories in Adulthood," *Psychological Science* 18, no. 5 (2007): 435–41, doi
.org/10.1111/j.1467-9280.2007.01918.x.

83 *for survivors of Nazi death camps*: Robert Kraft, *Memory Perceived: Recalling the Holocaust* (Westport, Conn.: Praeger, 2002).

83 *"Stronger emotional experiences make for stronger"*: James L. McGaugh,
quoted by B. Bower, "Stress Hormones Hike Emotional Memories,"
Science News 146, no. 17 (1994): 262, www.sciencenews.org/archive

/stress-hormones-hike-emotional-memories; James L. McGaugh, "Making Lasting Memories," *Proceedings of the National Academy of Sciences* 110, no. 2 (2013): 10402–7, doi.org/10.1073/pnas.1301209110.

17. WHEN FEAR OF LOSING STEALS OUR CHANCES OF WINNING

85 *curious attachment to what we have the* endowment effect: Daniel Kahneman, Jack L. Knetsch, and Richard H. Thaler, "Experimental Tests of the Endowment Effect and the Coase Theorem," *Journal of Political Economy* 98, no. 6 (1990): 1325–48, www.jstor.org/stable/2937761.

86 *it then continued production*: Glen Whyte, "Decision Failures: Why They Occur and How to Prevent Them," *Executive* 5, no. 3 (1991): 23–31, www.jstor.org/stable/4165019.

86 *"we could not simply walk away"*: John Lewis Gaddis, "Were the Hawks Right About the Vietnam War?," *Atlantic*, April 2000, www.theatlantic .com/magazine/archive/2000/04/were-the-hawks-right-about-the-viet nam-war/378155/.

86 *most people strongly prefer to lock in a profit*: Terrance Odean, "Are Investors Reluctant to Realize Their Losses?," *Journal of Finance* 53, no. 5 (1988): 1775–98, doi.org/10.1111/0022-1082.00072.

87 *we feel the pain from a loss*: Colin F. Camerer, "What Is Neuroeconomics?," Camerer Group, camerergroup.caltech.edu.

87 *a larger bad-is-stronger-than-good phenomenon*: Roy F. Baumeister et al., "Bad Is Stronger Than Good," *Review of General Psychology* 5, no. 4 (2001): 323–70, doi.org/10.1037//1089-2680.5.4.323.

87 *Most coaches, wanting to avoid a loss*: Roger Lowenstein, "Exuberance Is Rational," *New York Times Magazine*, March 4, 2001, www.nytimes .com/2001/03/04/magazine/l-exuberance-is-rational-105600.html.

88 *Similar loss aversion affects baseball*: Peter Macdonald, Don McQuillan, and Ian McQuillan, "Run for Third! A Defense of Aggressive Base Running," *Math Horizons* 23, no. 4 (2016): 14–15, doi.org/10.4169 /mathhorizons.23.4.14.

18. HOW WE POLARIZE, AND WHAT WE CAN DO ABOUT IT

90 *the percent of folks answering yes*: Douglas Barclay, "Democrats and Republicans Far Apart on Issues Ahead of Thanksgiving," PRRI, November 26, 2019, www.prri.org/spotlight/democrats-and-republicans-far -apart-on-issues-ahead-of-thanksgiving/.

92 *the result was group polarization*: David G. Myers and George D.

Bishop, "Discussion Effects on Racial Attitudes," *Science* 169, no. 3947 (1970): 778–79, doi.org/10.1126/science.169.3947.778.

92 *their group award tends to exceed*: Cass R. Sunstein, "Group Polarization and *12 Angry Men*," *Negotiation Journal* 23, no. 4 (2007): 443–47, doi .org/10.1111/j.1571-9979.2007.00155.x.

93 *polarization has deepened even among those*: Levi Boxell, Matthew Gentzkow, and Jesse M. Shapiro, "Is the Internet Causing Political Polarization?," NBER working paper, March 2017, doi.org/10.3386 /w23258.

94 *As Philip Bump reports*: Philip Bump, "How the Presidential Vote Has Evolved in Each County Since 2000," *Washington Post*, December 3, 2020, www.washingtonpost.com/politics/2020/12/03/how-presidential -vote-has-evolved-each-county-since-2000/.

94 *four in ten Biden and Trump supporters*: Amina Dunn, "Few Trump or Biden Supporters Have Close Friends Who Back the Opposing Candidate," Pew Research Center, September 18, 2020, www.pewresearch .org/fact-tank/2020/09/18/few-trump-or-biden-supporters-have-close -friends-who-back-the-opposing-candidate/.

94 *prioritizing Mark Zuckerberg's original vision*: Kimberlee Morrison, "Mark Zuckerberg: A Manifesto for Creating a More Connected World," *Ad Week*, August 22, 2013, www.adweek.com/performance-marketing /mark-zuckerberg-a-manifesto-for-creating-a-more-connected-world/.

94 *By flagging demonstrable untruths*: Elvira María Restrepo, "Online Technology as a Pathway for Citizen Deliberation and Depolarization," *Perspectives on Global Development and Technology* 17, no. 3 (2018): 239–63, brill.com/view/journals/pgdt/17/3/article-p239_2.xml?language=en.

94 *Nonprofit organizations working to depolarize America*: Living Room Conversations, livingroomconversations.org; the Civil Conversations Project, onbeing.org/civil-conversations-project/; the Depolarization Project, www.depolarizationproject.com; Braver Angels, braverangels.org.

95 *For some specific policies*: Ben White, "Soak the Rich? Americans Say Go for It," *Politico*, February 4, 2019, www.politico.com/story/2019/02 /04/democrats-taxes-economy-policy-2020-1144874; Harper Neidig, "Poll: 83 Percent of Voters Support Keeping FCC's Net Neutrality Rules," *The Hill*, December 12, 2017, thehill.com/policy/technology /364528-poll-83-percent-of-voters-support-keeping-fccs-net-neutrality

-rules; Leslie Davis and Hannah Hartig, "Two-Thirds of Americans Favor Raising Federal Minimum Wage to $15 an Hour," Pew Research Center, July 30, 2019, www.pewresearch.org/fact-tank/2019/07/30/two-thirds -of-americans-favor-raising-federal-minimum-wage-to-15-an-hour/.

19. OUR DIFFERENCES SEIZE OUR ATTENTION, DEFINE OUR IDENTITY, AND SOMETIMES DECEIVE US

97   *"insofar as, and in the ways that"*: W. J. McGuire et al., "Salience of Ethnicity in the Spontaneous Self-Concept as a Function of One's Ethnic Distinctiveness in the Social Environment," *Journal of Personality and Social Psychology* 36, no. 5 (1978): 511–20, doi.org/10.1037//0022-3514 .36.5.511.

97   *"being extremely or very important"*: Juliana Menasce Horowitz, Anna Brown, and Kiana Cox, "Race in America 2019," Pew Research Center, April 9, 2019, www.pewresearch.org/social-trends/2019/04/09/race-in -america-2019/.

98   *the experiment in which men*: Mark Snyder, Elizabeth Decker Tanke, and Ellen Berscheid, "Social Perception and Interpersonal Behavior: On the Self-Fulfilling Nature of Social Stereotypes," *Journal of Personality and Social Psychology* 35, no. 9 (1977): 656–66, psycnet.apa.org/doi /10.1037/0022–3514.35.9.656.

99   *in a follow-up experiment*: Robert D. Ridge and Jeffrey S. Reber, "'I Think She's Attracted to Me': The Effect of Men's Beliefs on Women's Behavior in a Job Interview Scenario," *Basic and Applied Social Psychology* 24, no. 1 (2002): 1–14, psycnet.apa.org/doi/10.1207 /153248302753439029.

99   *an ear-to-mouth facial scar*: Robert Kleck and Angelo Strenta, "Perceptions of the Impact of Negatively Valued Characteristics on Social Interaction," *Journal of Personality and Social Psychology* 39, no. 5 (1980): 861–73, doi.org/10.1037/0022-3514.39.5.861.

100 *Cornell University students were asked to don*: Thomas Gilovich, Victoria Husted Medvec, and Kenneth Savitsky, "The Spotlight Effect in Social Judgment: An Egocentric Bias in Estimates of the Salience of One's Own Actions and Appearance," *Journal of Personality and Social Psychology* 78, no. 2 (2000): 211–22, doi.org/10.1037/0022-3514.78.2.211.

20. THE PSYCHOLOGY OF DIVISION

104 *In studies by Henri Tajfel*: Henri Tajfel, "Experiments in Intergroup Discrimination," *Scientific American* 223, no. 5 (1970): 96–103, www.jstor .org/stable/24927662; Henri Tajfel, "Social Psychology of Intergroup Relations," *Annual Review of Psychology* 33 (1982): 1–39, doi.org/10 .1146/annurev.ps.33.020182.000245; Henri Tajfel and Michael Billig, "Familiarity and Categorization in Intergroup Behavior," *Journal of Experimental Psychology* 10, no. 2 (1974): 159–70.

104 *the psychologist Muzafer Sherif randomly split*: Muzafer Sherif, *In Common Predicament: Social Psychology of Intergroup Conflict and Cooperation* (Boston: Houghton Mifflin, 1966).

105 *The challenge is for cultures*: Fathali M. Moghaddam, "Omniculturalism: Policy Solutions to Fundamentalism in the Era of Fractured Globalization," *Culture and Psychology* 15, no. 13 (2009): 337–47, psycnet .apa.org/doi/10.1177/1354067X09337867.

21. THE SOCIAL PSYCHOLOGY OF DISSENT

106 *In a 1951 experiment*: Stanley Schachter, "Deviation, Rejection, and Communication," *Journal of Abnormal and Social Psychology* 46, no. 2 (1951): 190–207, psycnet.apa.org/doi/10.1037/h0062326.

106 *groups respond harshly to members*: Adam Rutland et al., "When Does the In-Group Like the Out-Group? Bias Among Children as a Function of Group Norms," *Psychological Science* 26, no. 6 (2015): 834–42, doi.org/10.1177%2F0956797615572758; Armelle Nugier et al., "Group Membership Influences Social Control of Perpetrators of Uncivil Behaviors," *European Journal of Social Psychology* 39, no. 6 (2007): 1126–34, doi.org/10.1002/ejsp.602.

107 *"for having kept so silent"*: Arthur M. Schlesinger Jr., *A Thousand Days* (Boston: Houghton Mifflin, 1965).

107 *"I don't like people who use"*: Ian Schwartz, "Trump Hits Romney at Prayer Breakfast: 'I Don't Like People Who Use Their Faith as Justification for Doing What They Know Is Wrong,'" Real Clear Politics, February 6, 2020, www.realclearpolitics.com/video/2020/02/06/trump _hits_romney_at_prayer_breakfast_i_dont_like_people_who_use_their _faith_as_justification_for_doing_what_they_know_is_wrong.html.

107 *"one of the worst campaigns"*: Meredith McGraw and Nancy Cook, "Trump's Impeachment Revenge List Starts with Romney," *Politico*, February 6, 2020, www.politico.com/news/2020/02/06/trump-mitt -romney-revenge-list-111789.

107 *Donald Trump Jr. went further*: Booker Brakkton, "Trump Blasts Romney over Impeachment Vote," NPR, February 6, 2020. www.npr.org /2020/02/06/803445433/trump-blasts-romney-over-impeachment-vote.

107 *Romney, some congressional colleagues derided*: Lee Zeldin (@RepLee Zeldin), Twitter, February 5, 2020, 2:21 p.m., twitter.com/RepLeeZeldin /status/1225137483706503168; Ledyard King, Maureen Groppe, and Christal Hayes, "GOP Sen. Romney Faces Awkwardness, 'Abuse' for Defying Trump on Impeachment," *USA Today*, February 6, 2020, www .usatoday.com/story/news/politics/2020/02/06/trump-impeachment -mitt-romney-braces-abuse-vote-convict/2859115001/; "Trump and Other Republicans Slam Romney over Impeachment Vote," Channel 3000, February 6, 2020, www.channel3000.com/trump-and-other -republicans-slam-romney-over-impeachment-vote/.

108 *wrote Ralph Waldo Emerson*: Ralph Waldo Emerson, Address read before the Phi Beta Kappa Society at Cambridge, July 18, 1867, www .bartleby.com/90/0807.html.

108 *In experiments, the French social psychologist*: Serge Moscovici, "Social Influence and Conformity," in *The Handbook of Social Psychology*, 3rd ed., ed. Gardner Lindzey and Elliot Aronson (Hillsdale, N.J.: Erlbaum, 1985); S. Moscovici, E. Lage, and M. Naffrechoux, "Influence of a Consistent Minority on the Responses of a Majority in a Color Perception Task," *Sociometry* 32, no. 4 (1969): 365–80, doi.org/10.2307 /2786541.

109 *The pain of being a dissenting minority*: John N. Bassili, "The Minority Slowness Effect: Subtle Inhibitions in the Expression of Views Not Shared by Others," *Journal of Personality and Social Psychology* 84, no. 2 (2003): 261–76, psycnet.apa.org/doi/10.1037/0022–3514.84.2.261.

109 *When the social psychologist Charlan Nemeth*: Charlan Jeanne Nemeth, "Minority Influence Theory," in *Handbook of Theories of Social Psychology*, ed. Paul A. M. van Lange, Arie W. Kruglanski, and E. Tory Higgins (Los Angeles: Sage, 2012), 2:362–78.

110 *But their consistency and charisma*: Robert J. House and Jitendra V.

Singh, "Organizational Behavior: Some New Directions for I/O Psychology," *Annual Review of Psychology* 38 (1987): 669–718, psycnet.apa .org/doi/10.1146/annurev.ps.38.020187.003321.

22. THE OVERCONFIDENCE PHENOMENON

111 *This wisdom, often attributed to*: Quote Investigator, quoteinvestigator .com/tag/stephen-hawking/.

112 *The social psychologist Philip Tetlock*: Philip E. Tetlock, *Expert Political Judgment: How Good Is It? How Can We Know?* (Princeton, N.J.: Princeton University Press, 2006).

112 *Paul Krugman has described similar overconfidence*: Paul Krugman, "The Doctrine of Trumpal Infallibility," *New York Times*, October 23, 2017, www.nytimes.com/2017/10/23/opinion/federal-reserve-john-taylor.html.

112 *conservative economists and pundits published*: Economics 21 Staff, "An Open Letter to Ben Bernanke," Economics 21, November 15, 2010, economics21.org/html/open-letter-ben-bernanke-287.html.

113 *Contacted by Bloomberg, not one*: Caleb Melby, Laura Marcinek, and Danielle Burger, "Fed Critics Say '10 Letter Warning Inflation Still Right," Bloomberg, October 2, 2014.

113 *A CivicScience poll asked*: Chris Baynes, "Most Americans Say 'Arabic Numerals' Should Not Be Taught in School, Finds Survey," *Independent*, May 21, 2019, www.independent.co.uk/news/arabic-numerals -survey-prejudice-bias-survey-research-civic-science-a8918256.html.

113 *Those who scored* lowest *on grammar*: Justin Kruger and David Dunning, "Unskilled and Unaware of It: How Difficulties in Recognizing One's Own Incompetence Lead to Inflated Self-Assessments," *Journal of Personality and Social Psychology* 77, no. 9 (1999): 1121–34, doi.org /10.1037//0022-3514.77.6.1121.

113 *"Our ignorance is invisible to us"*: Dunning, interview with Brian Resnick, "An Expert on Human Blindspots Gives Advice on How to Think," *Vox*, updated June 26, 2019, www.vox.com/science-and-health/2019/1 /31/18200497/dunning-kruger-effect-explained-trump.

114 *"blind to our [cognitive] blindness"*: Daniel Kahneman, "'We're Blind to Our Blindness. We Have Very Little Idea of How Little We Know. We're Not Designed To,'" *Independent*, November 24, 2011, www .independent.co.uk/arts-entertainment/books/features/we-re-blind

-our-blindness-we-have-very-little-idea-how-little-we-know-we-re-not
-designed-6267089.html.

114 *Robert Vallone and his colleagues*: Robert P. Vallone et al., "Overconfident Prediction of Future Actions and Outcomes by Self and Others," *Journal of Personality and Social Psychology* 58, no. 4 (1990): 582–92, psycnet.apa.org/doi/10.1037/0022–3514.58.4.582.

114 *seven in ten adults annually believe*: Art Swift, "Americans' Perceptions of U.S. Crime Problem Are Steady," Gallup, November 9, 2016, news.gallup .com/poll/197318/americans-perceptions-crime-problem-steady.aspx.

114 *fearmongering politicians may triumph*: Joshua D. Wright and Victoria M. Esses, "It's Security, Stupid! Voters' Perceptions of Immigrants as a Security Risk Predicted Support for Donald Trump in the 2016 US Presidential Election," *Journal of Applied Social Psychology* 49, no. 1 (2018): 36–49, doi.org/10.1111/jasp.12563.

114 *When immigrants crossing the southern U.S. border*: Jon Greenberg, "Donald Trump on the Campaign Trail: His Three Reasons to Fear Democrats, Fact-Checked," PolitiFact, October 8, 2018, www.politifact.com/article /2018/oct/08/trump-stump-his-reasons-fear-democrats-fact-checke/.

114 *lower actual crime and incarceration rates*: Michelangelo Landgrave and Alex Nowrasteh, "Incarcerated Immigrants in 2016: Their Numbers, Demographics, and Countries of Origin," Cato Institute, June 4, 2018, www.cato.org/sites/cato.org/files/pubs/pdf/irpb7.pdf.

114 *In 2021, unvaccinated people*: Gary Langer, "Vaccine-Hesitant Americans Reject Delta Variant Risk, Posing Questions for Pandemic Recovery," Yahoo! News, July 4, 2021, www.yahoo.com/gma/vaccine -hesitant-americans-reject-delta-040000508.html; Anthony Salvanto et al., "Biden Nets Positive Marks for Handling Pandemic, but Vaccine Resistance, Delta Concern Remains—CBS News Poll," CBS News, July 19, 2021, www.cbsnews.com/news/biden-pandemic-approval-covid-19 -opinion-poll/.

115 *As the late Hans Rosling*: Hans Rosling, *Factfulness*, with Ola Rosling and Anna Rosling Rönnlund (New York: Flatiron Books, 2018).

115 *Their vaccination estimate*: Max Roser, "New Entry on Vaccination Is Online—a New Survey Result Shows That We All Need to Update Our View on Vaccination," Our World in Data, October 18, 2018, ourworldindata.org/new-entry-on-vaccination.

115 *poverty has plummeted and literacy has soared*: Rosling, *Factfulness*.

115 *Students and construction planners often expect*: Roger Buehler, Dale Griffin, and Michael Ross, "Exploring the 'Planning Fallacy': Why People Underestimate Their Task Completion Times," *Journal of Personality and Social Psychology* 67, no. 3 (1994): 366–81, psycnet.apa.org /doi/10.1037/0022–3514.67.3.366.

115 *a week later than their "worst-case scenario"*: Roger Buehler, Dale Griffin, and Michael Ross, "Inside the Planning Fallacy: The Causes and Consequences of Optimistic Time Predictions," in *Heuristics and Biases: The Psychology of Intuitive Judgement*, ed. Thomas Gilovich, Dale W. Griffin, and Daniel Kahneman (Cambridge: Cambridge University Press, 2002), 250–70.

23. WHY IS EVERYONE ELSE HAVING MORE FUN?

117 *Across eleven studies, Cornell University's*: Sebastian Deri, Shai Davidai, and Thomas Gilovich, "Home Alone: Why People Believe Others' Social Lives Are Richer Than Their Own," *Journal of Personality and Social Psychology* 113, no. 6 (2017): 858–87, https://psycnet.apa.org/record /2017-52741-002.

118 *"research has empirically distinguished"*: Jenna L. Clark, Sara B. Algoe, and Melanie C. Green, "Social Network Sites and Well-Being: The Role of Social Connection," *Current Directions in Psychological Science* 27, no. 1 (2018), doi.org/10.1177/0963721417730833.

118 *moderate, interactive social media use*: Adam Waytz and Kurt Gray, "Does Online Technology Make Us More or Less Sociable? A Preliminary Review and Call for Research," *Perspectives on Psychological Science* 13, no. 4 (2018), doi.org/10.1177/1745691617746509.

118 *it's natural to feel a twinge of envy*: Philippe Verduyn et al., "Do Social Network Sites Enhance or Undermine Subjective Well-Being? A Critical Review," *Social Issues and Policy Review* 11, no. 1 (2017): 274–302, doi.org/10.1111/sipr.1203.

118 *When we see them having wonderful*: Ashley V. Whillans, Chelsea D. Christie, and Sarah Cheung, "From Misperception to Social Connection: Correlates and Consequences of Overestimating Others' Social Connectedness," *Personality and Social Psychology Bulletin* 43, no. 12 (2017), doi.org/10.1177/0146167217727496.

119 *American, Canadian, and British teen girls' rates*: Melissa C. Mercado, Kristin Holland, and Ruth W. Leemis, "Trends in Emergency Department Visits for Non-fatal Self-Inflicted Injuries Among Youth Aged 10 to 24 Years in the United States, 2001–2015," *JAMA* 318, no. 19 (2017): 1931–33, doi:10.1001/jama.2017.13317; Catharine Morgan et al., "Incidence, Clinical Management, and Mortality Risk Following Self Harm Among Children and Adolescents: Cohort Study in Primary Care," *BMJ* 4351 (2017): 359, doi.org/10.1136/bmj.j4351.

119 *In its follow-up monitoring*: "Explore Youth Risk Behavior Survey Questions—United States, 2019," Centers for Disease Control, yrbs-explorer.services.cdc.gov/#/.

120 *To explore a possible social media/depression connection*: Jonathan Haidt and Jean Twenge, "Social Media Use and Mental Health: A Review," MS (2021), New York University.

120 *"teens who visit"*: Jean Twenge, "Have Smartphones Destroyed a Generation?," *Atlantic*, September 2017.

121 *One recent study randomly assigned*: Hunt Allcott et al., "The Welfare Effects of Social Media," *American Economic Review* 110, no. 3 (2020): 629–76, 10.1257/aer.20190658.

121 *When internet use first soared*: R. Kraut et al., "Internet Paradox: A Social Technology That Reduces Social Involvement and Psychological Well-Being?," *American Psychology* 53, no. 9 (1998): 1017–103, https://psycnet.apa.org/buy/1998-10886-001.

121 *In one study, people estimated*: Sally Andrews et al., "Beyond Self-Report: Tools to Compare Estimated and Real-World Smartphone Use," *PLOS One* 10, no. 10 (2015), doi.org/10.1371/journal.pone.0139004.

122 *Haidt tweeted his recommendation*: Jonathan Haidt (@JonHaidt), Twitter, January 9, 2019, 7:21 a.m., twitter.com/JonHaidt/status/1083020940915757057.

122 *Twenge offered kindred advice for parents*: Jean M. Twenge, "Stop Debating Whether Too Much Smartphone Time Can Hurt Teens, and Start Protecting Them," *Time*, March 21, 2019, time.com/5555737/smartphone-mental-health-teens/.

122 *This scientific story is still being written*: Haidt and Twenge, "Social Media Use and Mental Health."

122 *But as Twenge summarizes*: Jean M. Twenge, "More Time on Technol-

ogy, Less Happiness? Associations Between Digital-Media Use and Psychological Well-Being," *Current Directions in Psychological Science* 28, no. 4 (2019), doi.org/10.1177/0963721419838244.

24. SOCIAL FACILITATION: THE ENERGIZING PRESENCE OF OTHERS

124 *"The bodily presence of another"*: Norman Triplett, "The Dynamogenic Factors in Pacemaking and Competition," *American Journal of Psychology* 9, no. 4 (1898): 507–33, doi.org/10.2307/1412188.

125 *at creative scientific moments*: Robert B. Zajonc, "Social Facilitation: A Solution Is Suggested for an Old Unresolved Social Psychological Problem," *Science* 149, no. 3681 (1965): 269–74, www.science.org/doi/10.1126/science.149.3681.269.

126 *would the solution survive direct experimental tests*: Charles F. Bond and Linda J. Titus, "A Meta-analysis of 241 Studies," *Psychological Bulletin* 94, no. 2 (1983): 265–92, psycnet.apa.org/doiLanding?doi=10.1037%2F0033-2909.94.2.265; Bernard Guerin, *Social Facilitation* (Cambridge: Cambridge University Press, 1993); Bernard Guerin, "Social Behaviors as Determined by Different Arrangements of Social Consequences: Social Loafing, Social Facilitation, Deindividuation, and a Modified Social Loafing," *Psychological Record* 49 (1999): 565–78.

126 *Social arousal produced by others' presence*: Peter Hunt and Joseph M. Hillery, "Social Facilitation in a Coaction Setting: An Examination of the Effects over Learning Trials," *Journal of Experimental Social Psychology* 9, no. 6 (1973): 563–71, www.sciencedirect.com/science/article/abs/pii/0022103173900383.

126 *Skilled student pool shooters*: J. W. Michaels et al., "Social Facilitation and Inhibition in a Natural Setting," *Replications in Social Psychology* 2 (1982): 21–24.

127 *contributes to the home advantage*: Marshall B. Jones, "The Home Advantage in Major League Baseball," *Perceptual and Motor Skills* 121, no. 3 (2015): 791–804, journals.sagepub.com/doi/10.2466/26.PMS.121c25x1.

127 *So what happened during the pandemic*: Rory Smith, "Do Empty Stadiums Affect Outcomes? The Data Says Yes," *New York Times*, July 1, 2020; Michael C. Leitner and Fabio Richlan, "No Fans—No Pressure: Referees in Professional Football During the COVID-19 Pandemic,"

Frontiers in Sports and Active Living, August 19, 2021, doi.org/10.3389
/fspor.2021.720488.

127 *fun shared with others is distinctly more energizing*: Jonathan Freedman
and Deborah Perlick, "Crowding, Contagion, and Laughter," *Journal of
Experimental Social Psychology* 15, no. 3 (1979): 295–303, doi.org/10
.1016/0022-1031(79)90040-4.

127 *people have had higher pulse rates*: Gary W. Evans, "Behavioral and Phys-
iological Consequences of Crowding in Humans," *Journal of Applied
Social Psychology* 9, no. 1 (1979): 27–46, doi.org/10.1111/j.1559-1816
.1979.tb00793.x.

25. THE HAPPY SCIENCE OF MICRO-FRIENDSHIPS

130 *with fewer pandemic-era face-to-face meetings*: David Myers, "COVID
and the Mental Health of People Young and Old," *Talk Psych* (blog),
April 20, 2020, community.macmillanlearning.com/t5/talk-psych-blog
/covid-and-the-mental-health-of-people-young-and-old/ba-p/689.

130 *The University of British Columbia researchers*: Gillian M. Sandstrom
and Elizabeth W. Dunn, "Is Efficiency Overrated? Minimal Social
Interactions Lead to Belonging and Positive Affect," *Social Psychological and Personality Science*, September 12, 2013, doi.org/10.1177
/1948550613502990.

130 *In multiple experiments*: Nicholas Epley and Juliana Schroeder, "Mistakenly Seeking Solitude," *Journal of Experimental Psychology: General*
143, no. 5 (2014): 1980–999, doi.org/10.1037/a0037323.

131 *In five experiments*: Erica Boothby and Vanessa K. Bohns, "Why a Simple
Act of Kindness Is Not as Simple as It Seems: Underestimating the Positive Impact of Our Compliments on Others," *Personality and Social Psychology Bulletin*, Aug. 28, 2020, doi.org/10.1177/0146167220949003.

131 *To pin down cause and effect*: Gul Gunaydin et al., "Minimal Social Interactions with Strangers Predict Greater Subjective Well-Being," *Journal of Happiness Studies* 22 (2021): 1839–53, doi.org/10.1007/s10902
-020-00298-6.

26. HOW TO MAKE AND SUSTAIN FRIENDSHIPS

136 *"Everyone's existence is deeply tied"*: Pope Francis, "Why the Only Future Worth Building Includes Everyone," trans. Elena Montrasio, TED

Talk, April 2017, www.ted.com/talks/pope_francis_why_the_only
_future_worth_building_includes_everyone/transcript?language=en.

136 *About 150 people, contends the retired*: David Myers, "How Many
Friends Do You Have?," *Talk Psych* (blog), August 9, 2021, commu
nity.macmillanlearning.com/t5/talk-psych-blog/how-many-friends-do
-you-have/ba-p/15275.

137 *Longing for approval, acceptance, and love*: M. Ridder, "Leading Cos-
metics & Personal Care Products Markets Worldwide 2018, by Reve-
nue," Statista, November 23, 2020, www.statista.com/statistics/717673
/cosmetics-personal-care-products-markets-revenue/.

138 *Indeed, in a deepening relationship*: Margaret S. Clark and Judson Mills,
"The Difference Between Communal and Exchange Relationships:
What It Is and Is Not," *Personality and Social Psychology Bulletin* 19, no.
6 (1993), doi.org/10.1177/0146167293196003.

139 *As one Pew Research Center report*: "Modern Marriage," Pew Research
Center, July 18, 2017, www.pewresearch.org/social-trends/2007/07/18
/modern-marriage/.

139 *The social psychologist Arthur Aron*: Arthur Aron et al., "The Experimental Generation of Interpersonal Closeness: A Procedure and
Some Preliminary Findings," *Personality and Social Psychology Bulletin* 23, no. 4 (1997): 365–77, journals.sagepub.com/doi/pdf/10.1177
/0146167297234003.

140 *And those whose days more often include*: Matthias R. Mehl et al., "Eaves-
dropping on Happiness: Well-Being Is Related to Having Less Small
Talk and More Substantive Conversations," *Psychological Science* 21,
no. 4 (2010): 539–41, doi.org/10.1177/0956797610362675.

140 *Some people are especially skilled*: Linda J. Pegalis et al., "On the Abil-
ity to Elicit Self-Disclosure: Are There Gender-Based and Contextual
Limitations on the Opener Effect?," *Personality and Social Psychology
Bulletin* 20, no. 4 (1994), doi.org/10.1177/0146167294204008.

140 *During conversation, they maintain*: James A. Purvis, James M. Dabbs
Jr., and Charles H. Hopper, "The 'Opener': Skilled User of Facial Expression and Speech Pattern," *Personality and Social Psychology Bulletin*
10, no. 1 (1984), doi.org/10.1177/0146167284101006.

140 *In his classic*: Dale Carnegie, *How to Win Friends and Influence People*
(New York: Simon & Schuster, 1936).

141 *the marriage researcher John Gottman*: John M. Gottman, *The Marriage Clinic: A Scientifically Based Marital Therapy* (New York: Norton Professional Books, 1999).

141 *Then he followed their marriage*: Kyle Benson, "The Magic Relationship Ratio, According to Science," Gottman Institute, Oct. 1, 2017, www.gottman.com/blog/the-magic-relationship-ratio-according-science.

141 *As Roy Baumeister*: Roy F. Baumeister et al., "Bad Is Stronger Than Good," *Review of General Psychology* 5, no. 4 (2001), doi.org/10.1037/1089-2680.5.4.323.

27. NARCISSISM: THE GRANDIOSE SELF

142 *To study narcissists' reactions to criticism*: Brad J. Bushman and Roy F. Baumeister, "Threatened Egotism, Narcissism, Self-Esteem, and Direct and Displaced Aggression: Does Self-Love or Self-Hate Lead to Violence?," *Journal of Personality and Social Psychology* 75, no. 1 (1998): 219–29.

143 *Narcissists may be charming*: Brad J. Bushman et al., "Looking Again, and Harder, for a Link Between Low Self-Esteem and Aggression," *Journal of Personality* 77, no. 2 (2009): 427–46, doi.org/10.1111/j.1467-6494.2008.00553.x.

143 *narcissists have often come from homes*: Eddie Brummelman et al., "Origins of Narcissism in Children," *Proceedings of the Natural Academy of Sciences* 112, no. 12 (2015): 3659–62.

144 *They tend to be very active*: Timo Gnambs and Markus Appel, "Narcissism and Social Networking Behavior: A Meta-analysis," *Journal of Personality* 86, no. 2 (2017): 200–212, doi.org/10.1111/jopy.12305; Dong Liu and Roy F. Baumeister, "Social Networking Online and Personality of Self-Worth: A Meta-analysis," *Journal of Research in Personality* 64 (2016): 79–89, doi.org/10.1016j.jrp.2016.06.024; Jessica L. McCain and W. Keith Campbell, "Narcissism and Social Media Use: A Meta-analytic Review," *Psychology of Popular Media Culture* 7, no. 3 (2018): 308–27, doi.org/10.1037/ppm0000137.

144 *those scoring high in narcissism*: Amy B. Brunell et al., "Leader Emergence: The Case of the Narcissistic Leader, " *Personality and Social Psychology Bulletin* 34 (2008): 1663–76, doi.org/10.1177/0146167208324101.

144 *their popularity declined as group members*: Marius Leckelt et al., "Be-

havioral Processes Underlying the Decline of Narcissists' Popularity over Time," *Journal of Personality and Social Psychology* 109, no. 5 (2015): 856–71, doi.org/10.1037/pspp0000057.

28. HOW NATURE AND NURTURE FORM US

150 *In study after study*: Tena Vukasovic and Denis Bratko, "Heritability of Personality: A Meta-analysis of Behavior Genetic Studies," *Psychological Bulletin* 141, no. 4 (2015): 769–85, doi:10.1037/bul0000017.

151 *Nancy Segal seized this opportunity*: Nancy L. Segal, "Personality Similarity in Unrelated Look-Alike Pairs: Addressing a Twin Study Challenge," *Personality and Individual Differences* 54, no. 1 (2013): 23–28, doi.org/10.1016/j.paid.2012.07.031.

151 *In a follow-up study*: Nancy L. Segal, Jamie L. Graham, and Ulrich Ettinger, "Unrelated Look-Alikes: Replicated Study of Personality Similarity and Qualitative Findings on Social Relatedness," *Personality and Individual Differences* 55, no. 2 (2013): 169–74, doi.org/10.1016/j.paid.2013.02.024.

151 *"We would essentially be the same person"*: Robert Plomin, "In the Nature-Nurture War, Nature Wins," *Scientific American* (blog), December 14, 2018, blogs.scientificamerican.com/observations/in-the-nature-nurture-war-nature-wins/.

152 *A University of Minnesota team*: Emily A. Willoughby et al., "Free Will, Determinism, and Intuitive Judgments About the Heritability of Behavior," Department of Psychology, University of Minnesota Twin Cities, Minneapolis, osf.io/ezg2j/.

29. THE WONDER OF WALKING (AND SINGING): SYNCHRONIZED SPIRITS

154 *"walking together can facilitate both"*: Christine E. Webb, Maya Rossignac-Milon, and E. Tory Higgins, "Stepping Forward Together: Could Walking Facilitate Interpersonal Conflict Resolution?," *American Psychologist* 72, no. 4 (2017): 374–85, doi:10.1037/a0040431.

155 *Sitting at a wobbly desk and chair*: Amanda L. Forest et al., "Turbulent Times, Rocky Relationships: Relational Consequences of Experiencing Physical Instability," *Psychological Science* 26, no. 8 (2015), doi.org/10.1177/0956797615586402.

155   *On a warm day*: Adam K. Fetterman, Benjamin M. Wilowski, and Michael D. Robinson, "On Feeling Warm and Being Warm: Daily Perceptions of Physical Warmth Fluctuate with Interpersonal Warmth," *Social Psychological and Personality Science* 9, no. 5 (2018), doi.org/10.1177/1948550617712032.

155   *Sitting on a hard rather than soft*: Michael Schaefer et al., "Incidental Haptic Sensations Influence Judgment of Crimes," *Scientific Reports* 8, no. 6039 (2018), doi.org/10.1038/s41598-018-23586-x.

155   *Striding with head high and shoulders back*: Dana R. Carney, Amy J. C. Cuddy, and Andy J. Yap, "Review and Summary of Research on the Embodied Effects of Expansive (vs. Contractive) Nonverbal Displays," *Psychological Science* 26, no. 5 (2015), doi.org/10.1177/0956797614566855.

156   *Empathic mimicking—as when a listener nods*: Tanya L. Chartrand and Rick Van Baaren, "Human Mimicry," in *Advances in Experimental Social Psychology*, ed. Mark P. Zanna (Boston: Elsevier, 2009), 41:219–74.

156   *We not only mirror the movements*: Maike Salazar Kampf et al., "Disentangling the Sources of Mimicry: Social Relations Analyses of the Link Between Mimicry and Liking," *Psychological Science* 29, no. 1 (2018), doi.org/10.1177/0956797617727121.

156   *Biologists who study herding*: Simone G. Shamay-Tsoory et al., "Herding Brains: A Core Neural Mechanism for Social Alignment," *Trends in Cognitive Sciences* 23, no. 3 (2019): 174–86, doi.org/10.1016/j.tics.2019.01.002.

156   *Perhaps for our early ancestors*: Liam Cross, "Walk in My Shoes," *Psychologist* 33 (2020): 24–27, thepsychologist.bps.org.uk/volume-33/june-2020/walk-my-shoes.

30. WISE INTERVENTIONS CAN CHANGE LIVES

158   *When Joan McCord*: Joan McCord and William McCord, "A Follow-Up Report on the Cambridge-Somerville Youth Study," *Annals of the American Academy of Political and Social Science* 322, no. 1 (1959), doi.org/10.1177/000271625932200112.

159   *The most comprehensive review of twin studies*: Tinca J. C. Polderman et al., "Meta-analysis of the Heritability of Human Traits Based on Fifty Years of Twin Studies," *Nature Genetics* 47 (2015): 702–709, doi.org/10.1038/ng.3285.

159 *Given the guiding power of our heredity*: Gregory M. Walton and Timothy D. Wilson, "Wise Interventions: Psychological Remedies for Social and Personal Problems," *Psychological Review* 125, no. 5 (2018): 617–55, doi.org/10.1037/rev0000115.

160 *At-risk middle school students*: Carol S. Dweck, Gregory M. Walton, and Geoffrey L. Cohen, "Academic Tenacity: Mindsets and Skills That Promote Long-Term Learning," Bill and Melinda Gates Foundation (2014), ed.stanford.edu/sites/default/files/manual/dweck-walton -cohen-2014.pdf.

160 *Entering minority college students*: Gregory M. Walton and Geoffrey L. Cohen, "A Brief Social-Belonging Intervention Improves Academic and Health Outcomes of Minority Students," *Science* 331, no. 1447 (2011): doi:10.1126/science.1198364; Lisa Quay, "The Science of 'Wise Interventions': Applying a Social Psychological Perspective to Address Problems and Help People Flourish," *Research Summary*, August 2018, studentexperiencenetwork.org/wp-content/uploads/2018/08 /The-Science-of-Wise-Interventions.pdf.

161 *despite college administrators' frustrated past efforts*: D. S. Yeager et al., "Teaching a Lay Theory Before College Narrows Achievement Gaps at Scale," *Proceedings of the National Academy of Sciences* 113, no. 24 (2016), doi.org/10.1073/pnas.1524360113.

31. FAILURE AND FLOURISHING

163 *So why not make our setbacks*: Melanie Stefan, "A CV of Failures," *Nature* 468, no. 467 (2010), doi.org/10.1038/nj7322-467a.

163 *Stefan inspired the Stockholm University economist*: Johannes Haushofer, Curriculum Vitae, haushofer.ne.su.se.

163 *The neuroscientist Bradley Voytek*: Bradley Voytek, Vitae, voyteklab.com.

164 Rejection *is the apt title*: John White, *Rejection* (Boston: Addison-Wesley, 1982).

164 *Such stories continue to accumulate*: Alison Flood, "JK Rowling Says She Received 'Loads' of Rejections Before Harry Potter Success," *Guardian* (blog), March 24, 2015, www.theguardian.com/books/2015/mar /24/jk-rowling-tells-fans-twitter-loads-rejections-before-harry-potter -success; Danny Hajek, "How'd a Cartoonist Sell His First Drawing? It Only Took 610 Tries," *My Big Break*, NPR, January 25, 2015, www.npr

.org/2015/01/25/379787274/howd-a-cartoonist-sell-his-first-drawing-it
-only-took-610-tries; Hillel Italie, "Not So Fast: Many Nobel Winners
Endured Initial Rejections," AP News, October 14, 2019, apnews.com
/article/entertainment-science-us-news-a85ac210de58448797735d7d5b0
4779c.

165 *If, as John Gottman has long reported*: Kyle Benson, "The Magic Relationship Ratio, According to Science," Gottman Institute, October 4,
2017, www.gottman.com/blog/the-magic-relationship-ratio-according
-science/.

167 *"Twenty-six times I've been trusted"*: Mark Selig, "Michael Jordan's Top
23 Commercials, Remembered and Ranked," *Washington Post*, April 27,
2020, www.washingtonpost.com/sports/2020/04/27/michael-jordan
-commercials/.

32. DEATH IS TERRIFYING TO CONTEMPLATE, EXCEPT FOR THOSE WHO ARE DYING

169 *And now comes a third striking*: Amelia Goranson et al., "Dying Is Unexpectedly Positive," *Psychological Science* 28, no. 1 (2017): 988–99,
doi:10.1177/0956797617701186.

170 *The first of 2,632 posts*: Amelia Goranson, "Terminal Illness Blog Posts"
(2017), dataverse.unc.edu/dataset.xhtml?persistentId=doi:10.15139/S3
/PYAQWQ.

172 *Goranson and her colleagues presume*: Andrew Reed and Laura L.
Carstensen, "The Theory Behind the Age-Related Positivity Effect," *Frontiers in Psychology* 339, no. 3 (2012), doi:10.3389/fpsyg.2012.00339.

172 *And so it was for the civil rights legend*: John Lewis, "Together, You Can
Redeem the Soul of Our Nation," *New York Times*, July 30, 2020, www
.nytimes.com/2020/07/30/opinion/john-lewis-civil-rights-america.html.

33. DO PLACES WITH MORE IMMIGRANTS EXHIBIT GREATER ACCEPTANCE OR GREATER FEAR OF IMMIGRANTS?

173 *President Trump repeatedly told*: Amber Phillips, "'They're Rapists': President Trump's Campaign Launch Speech Two Years Later, Annotated,"
Washington Post, June 16, 2017, www.washingtonpost.com/news/the
-fix/wp/2017/06/16/theyre-rapists-presidents-trump-campaign-launch
-speech-two-years-later-annotated/.

173 *At a West Virginia rally*: Darran Simon, "Politicians Blame Immigration Laws for Mollie Tibbetts' Fate," CNN, August 22, 2018, www.cnn.com /2018/08/21/us/mollie-tibbetts-missing-iowa-student-murder-suspect /index.html.

174 *At a Sydney symposium*: Christian Unkelbach, Vitae, soccco.uni-koeln .de/christian-unkelbach.

174 *might a similar pattern*: Ulrich Wagner et al., "Proportion of Foreigners Negatively Predicts the Prevalence of Xenophobic Hate Crimes Within German Districts," *Social Psychology Quarterly* 83, no. 2 (2020), doi.org /10.1177/0190272519887719.

174 *A 2016 Pew report*: "U.S. Unauthorized Immigrant Population Estimates by State, 2016," Pew Research Center, February 5, 2019, www.pewresearch .org/hispanic/interactives/u-s-unauthorized-immigrants-by-state/.

174 *A 2016 PRRI "American Values" report*: "The Cultural Impact of Immigrants," *PRRI American Values Atlas* (2015), www.prri.org/wp-content /uploads/2016/03/CHART-5-1.jpg.

175 *In a new article at age eighty-seven*: Thomas F. Pettigrew, "The Emergence of Contextual Social Psychology," *Personality and Social Psychology Bulletin* 44, no. 7 (2018), doi.org/10.1177/0146167218756033.

34. IMPLICIT BIAS IS REAL. CAN TRAINING PROGRAMS DECREASE IT?

178 *Was this but "an isolated incident"*: "HuffPost: Starbucks Controversy," April 19, 2018, big.assets.huffingtonpost.com/athena/files/2018/04 /23/5addfc31e4b0b2e81131eb0a.pdf.

178 *After Amadou Diallo was shot*: Joshua Correll et al., "Stereotypic Vision: How Stereotypes Disambiguate Visual Stimuli," *Journal of Personality and Social Psychology* 108, no. 2 (2015): 219–33, doi:10.1037 /pspa0000015.

179 *Outside the laboratory*: Marianne Bertrand and Sendhil Mullainathan, "Are Emily and Greg More Employable Than Lakisha and Jamal? A Field Experiment on Labor Market Discrimination," *American Economic Review* 94, no. 4 (2004): 991–1013, www.jstor.org/stable/3592802.

179 *As if aware of the result*: "Transcript: Obama Delivers Eulogy for Charleston Pastor, the Rev. Clementa Pinckney," *Washington Post*, June 26, 2015, www.washingtonpost.com/news/post-nation/wp/2015

/06/26/transcript-obama-delivers-eulogy-for-charleston-pastor-the
-rev-clementa-pinckney/.

179 *Similar racial disparities have been found*: Benjamin Edelman, Michael
Luca, and Dan Svirsky, "Racial Discrimination in the Sharing Econ-
omy: Evidence from a Field Experiment," *American Economic Journal:
Applied Economics* 9, no. 2 (2017): 1–22, doi:10.1257/app.20160213;
Yanbo Ge et al., "Racial and Gender Discrimination in Transportation
Network Companies," National Bureau of Economic Research, Octo-
ber 2016, doi:10.3386/w22776.

179 *driver treatment during police traffic stops*: Rob Voigt et al., "Language
from Police Body Camera Footage Shows Racial Disparities in Officer
Respect," *Proceedings of the National Academy of Sciences* 114, no. 25
(2017): 6521–26, doi.org/10.1073/pnas.1702413114.

179 *Across 217 studies, implicit reactions*: Benedek Kurdi et al., "Relationship Between the Implicit Association Test and Intergroup Behavior: A
Meta-analysis," *American Psychologist* 74, no. 5 (2019): 569–86, doi.org
/10.1037/amp0000364.

180 *Skeptics argue that "blame and shame"*: Frank Dobbin and Alexandra
Kalev, "Why Diversity Programs Fail," *Harvard Business Review*, July–
August 2016, hbr.org/2016/07/why-diversity-programs-fail.

180 *"implicit bias training . . . has not been shown"*: Katie Herzog, "Is Starbucks
Implementing Flawed Science in Their Anti-bias Training?," *Stranger*,
April 17, 2018, www.thestranger.com/slog/2018/04/17/26052277/is
-starbucks-implementing-flawed-science-in-their-anti-bias-training.

180 *"diversity trainings are filled"*: Julia Belluz, "Companies Like Starbucks
Love Anti-bias Training. But It Doesn't Work—and May Backfire,"
Vox, May 29, 2018, www.vox.com/science-and-health/2018/4/19
/17251752/philadelphia-starbucks-arrest-racial-bias-training.

180 *research on automatic prejudice*: Patricia G. Devine et al., "Long-Term
Reduction in Implicit Race Bias: A Prejudice Habit-Breaking Intervention," *Journal of Experimental Social Psychology* 48, no. 6 (2012): 1267–
78, doi:10.1016/j.jesp.2012.06.003.

180 *Another team of twenty-four researchers*: Calvin K. Lai et al., "Reducing Implicit Racial Preferences: I. A Comparative Investigation of 17
Interventions," *Journal of Experimental Psychology: General* 143, no. 4
(2014): 1765–85, doi:10.1037/a0036260.

181 *Nosek and Devine collaborated*: Patrick S. Forscher et al., "A Meta-analysis of Procedures to Change Implicit Measures," *Journal of Personality and Social Psychology* 117, no. 1 (2019): 522–59, doi:10.1037/pspa0000160.

181 *Neuroscience evidence shows*: William A. Cunningham et al., "Separable Neural Components in the Processing of Black and White Faces," *Psychological Science* 15, no. 12 (2004): 806–13, doi:10.1111/j.0956-7976.2004.00760.x.

181 *As the race expert Charles Green explains*: "The ABCs of Inclusion," Hope College Blog Network, blogs.hope.edu/getting-race-right/our-options-where-we-go-from-here/making-a-difference/the-abcs-of-inclusion/.

35. HOW POLITICS CHANGES POLITICIANS

183 *How did Ted Cruz's 2016 assessment*: David Wright, Tal Kopan, and Julia Manchester, "Cruz Unloads with Epic Takedown of 'Pathological Liar,' 'Narcissist' Donald Trump," CNN Politics, May 3, 2016, www.cnn.com/2016/05/03/politics/donald-trump-rafael-cruz-indiana/index.html.

183 *Carl Bernstein could name*: Martin Pengelly, "Bernstein Names 21 Republican Senators Who Privately Expressed Contempt for Trump," *Guardian*, November 23, 2020, www.theguardian.com/us-news/2020/nov/23/carl-bernstein-21-republican-senators-expressed-contempt-for-trump.

184 *And no more do we hear*: Zohreen Shah, "Sen. Kamala Harris Doubles Down on Criticism of Biden's Busing Comments on *The View*," July 12, 2020, abcnews.go.com/Politics/sen-kamala-harris-view-doubles-criticism-bidens-busing/story?id=64243647.

184 *We are quicker to tell*: Melvin Manis, S. Douglas Cornell, and Jeffrey C. Moore, "Transmission of Attitude Relevant Information Through a Communication Chain," *Journal of Personality and Social Psychology* 30, no. 1 (1974): 81–94, doi.org/10.1037/h0036639.

184 *people have been observed to adapt*: E. Tory Higgins and C. Douglas McCann, "Social Encoding and Subsequent Attitudes, Impressions, and Memory: 'Context-Driven' and Motivational Aspects of Processing," *Journal of Personality and Social Psychology* 47, no. 1 (1984): 26–39, doi.org/10.1037/0022-3514.47.1.26.

184 *The retired University of Oregon psychologist*: Ray Hyman, "'Cold

Reading': How to Convince Strangers That You Know All About Them," *Skeptical Inquirer* 1, no. 2 (1977), skepticalinquirer.org/1977/04/cold -reading-how-to-convince-strangers-that-you-know-all-about-them/.

185 *"You can use small commitments"*: Robert B. Cialdini, *Influence: The Psychology of Persuasion* (New York: Harper Business, 2006).

185 *"are too strong for them"*: Ralph Waldo Emerson, "Representative Men," *Essays and Lectures* (New York: Penguin Putnam, 1983), 749, en.wikisource .org/wiki/Representative_Men/Goethe;_or,_the_Writer.

185 *After inducing Richard Rich*: Robert Bolt, *A Man for All Seasons: A Play of Sir Thomas More* (Scarborough, Ont.: Belhaven House, 1968).

186 *In a 1944 lecture*: C. S. Lewis, "The Inner Ring," in *The Weight of Glory* (Grand Rapids, Mich.: Eerdmans, 1965), 61–64.

36. THE POWER OF CONFIRMATION BIAS
AND THE CREDIBILITY OF BELIEF

188 *"the sheer scale of the belief"*: Ross Douthat, "Why Do So Many Americans Think the Election Was Stolen?," *New York Times*, December 5, 2020, www.nytimes.com/2020/12/05/opinion/sunday/trump-election -fraud.html.

188 *In a pioneering study*: P. C. Wason, "On the Failure to Eliminate Hypotheses in a Conceptual Task," *Quarterly Journal of Experimental Psychology* 12, no. 3 (1960): 129–40, doi:10.1080/17470216008416717.

189 *In several experiments*: Mark Snyder and William B. Swann, "Hypothesis-Testing Processes in Social Interaction," *Journal of Personality and Social Psychology* 36, no. 11 (1978): 1202–12, doi.org/10.1037/0022-3514 .36.11.1202.

190 *Across various issues, both conservatives*: Jeremy A. Frimer, Linda J. Skitka, and Matt Motyl, "Liberals and Conservatives Are Similarly Motivated to Avoid Exposure to One Another's Opinions," *Journal of Experimental Social Psychology* 72 (2017): 1–12, doi.org/10.1016/j.jesp .2017.04.003.

190 *Robert Browning understood*: Robert Browning, *The Poetical Works of Robert Browning*, vol. 5, *Dramatic Romances; Christmas-Eve and Easter Day* (London: Macmillan, 1903).

190 *Confirmation bias supplements another idea*: C. A. Anderson, M. R. Lepper, and L. Ross, "The Perseverance of Social Theories: The Role of

Explanation in the Persistence of Discredited Information," *Journal of Personality and Social Psychology* 39, no. 6 (1980): 1037–49, doi.org/10 .1037/h0077720.

192 *Archbishop William Temple recognized*: Michael W. Poole, *Beliefs and Values in Science Education* (Oxford: Marston Book Services, 1995), 24.

193 *As Saint Paul advised*: 1 Thessalonians 5:21.

37. FRIENDS VERSUS PHONES

194 *In one small survey*: James Roberts and Meredith David, "My Life Has Become a Major Distraction from My Cell Phone: Partner Phubbing and Relationship Satisfaction Among Romantic Partners," *Computers in Human Behavior* 54 (January 2016): 134–41, doi.org/10.1016/j.chb .2015.07.058.

194 *That result would not surprise*: David A. Sbarra, Julia L. Briskin, and Richard B. Slatcher, "Smartphones and Close Relationships: The Case for an Evolutionary Mismatch," *Perspectives on Psychological Science* 14, no. 4 (2019): doi.org/10.1177/1745691619826535.

195 *A study by Ryan Dwyer*: Ryan J. Dwyer, Kostadin Kushlev, and Elizabeth W. Dunn, "Smartphone Use Undermines Enjoyment of Face-to-face Social Interactions," *Journal of Experimental Social Psychology* 78 (2018): 233–39, doi.org/10.1016/j.jesp.2017.10.007.

195 *They invited students to put*: Varoth Chotpitayasunondh and Karen M. Douglas, "The Effects of 'Phubbing' on Social Interaction," *Journal of Applied Social Psychology* 48, no. 6 (2018): 304–16, doi.org/10.1111 /jasp.12506.

38. WEALTH, WELL-BEING, AND GENEROSITY

198 *In the most recent UCLA*: Kevin Eagan et al., "The American Freshman: National Norms Fall 2016," Higher Education Research Institute, UCLA (2017).

198 *For individuals in poor countries*: Andrew T. Jebb et al., "Happiness, Income Satiation, and Turning Points Around the World," *Nature Human Behavior* 2 (2018): 33–38, doi.org/10.1038/s41562-017-0277-0.

199 *In many countries, including the United States, China, and India*: Joe Hasell, "Is Income Inequality Rising Around the World?," Our World in Data, November 19, 2018, ourworldindata.org/income-inequality-since-1990.

200 *The number of "very happy" adults*: Andrea Weinberger et al., "Depression Is on the Rise in the U.S., Especially Among Young Teens," Child and Adolescent Health, Columbia, October 30, 2017, www .publichealth.columbia.edu/public-health-now/news/depression-rise-us -especially-among-young-teens.

200 Our tendency to assess our own circumstances: J. P. Gerber, Ladd Wheeler, and Jerry Suls, "A Social Comparison Theory Meta-analysis 60+ Years On," *Psychological Bulletin* 144, no. 2 (2017): 177–97, doi:10.1037/bul0000127.

200 *People with a $40,000 income*: Robert Frank, "What Does It Take to Feel Wealthy?," *Inside Wealth*, July 19, 2012, www.cnbc.com/id/48240956.

200 *The outer limit of the relationship*: Grant E. Donnelly et al., "The Amount and Source of Millionaires' Wealth (Moderately) Predict Their Happiness," *Personality and Social Psychology Bulletin* 44, no. 5 (2018): 684–99, doi:10.1177/0146167217744766.

201 *In nations or states with greater inequality*: Keith Payne, *The Broken Ladder: How Inequality Affects the Way We Think, Live, and Die* (London: Penguin, 2018); Nicolas Sommet, Davide Morselli, and Dario Spini, "Income Inequality Affects the Psychological Health of Only the People Facing Scarcity," *Psychological Science* 29, no. 12 (2018), doi.org/10 .1177/0956797618798620; Richard Wilkinson and Kate Pickett, "Inequality and Mental Illness," *Lancet Psychiatry* 4, no. 7 (2017): 512–13, doi.org/10.1016/S2215-0366(17)30206-7.

201 *Regardless of politics, most people*: William F. Arsenio, "The Wealth of Nations: International Judgments Regarding Actual and Ideal Resource Distributions," *Current Directions in Psychological Science* 27, no. 5 (2018), doi.org/10.1177/0963721418762377.

201 *Moreover, those most materialistic*: Grant E. Donnelly et al., "Buying to Blunt Negative Feelings: Materialistic Escape from the Self," *Review of General Psychology* 20, no. 3 (2016), doi.org/10.1037/gpr0000078.

201 *Those who instead prioritize intimacy*: Tim Kasser, "Materialism and Living Well," in *Handbook of Well-Being*, ed. Ed Diener, Shigehiro Oishi, and Louis Tay (Salt Lake City: DEF, 2018), doi:nobascholar.com.

201 *If wealth increases well-being*: Richard Wilkinson and Kate Pickett, "The Science Is In: Greater Equality Makes Societies Healthier and Richer,"

Evonomics, evonomics.com/wilkinson-pickett-income-inequality-fix
-economy/.

201 *Let's make this personal*: Isaiah 55:2.

39. THE MERE EXPOSURE EFFECT: FAMILIARITY BREEDS CONTENT

203 *"If it's familiar"*: Drake Bennett, "How 'Cognitive Fluency' Shapes
What We Believe, How We Invest, and Who Will Become a Super-
model," *Boston Globe*, January 31, 2010.

204 *When Zajonc showed University of Michigan students*: Robert B. Zajonc,
"Attitudinal Effects of Mere Exposure," *Journal of Personality and Social
Psychology* 9, no. 2, part 2 (1968).

206 *In an experiment, they preferred*: Eddie Harmon-Jones and John J. B.
Allen, "The Role of Affect in the Mere Exposure Effect: Evidence from
Psychophysiological and Individual Differences Approaches," *Personality and Social Psychology Bulletin* 27, no. 7 (2001): 889–98, doi.org/10
.1177/0146167201277011.

206 *When candidates are unknown, media exposure*: Thomas E. Patterson,
"The Role of the Mass Media in Presidential Campaigns: The Lessons of
the 1976 Election," *Items* 34, no. 2 (1980): 25–30, www.semanticscholar
.org/paper/The-Mass-Media-Election%3A-How-Americans-Choose
-Their-Patterson/8b0781bf9a1020176f5a73bf8124cb5851246928.

40. DO REPLICATION FAILURES DISCREDIT PSYCHOLOGICAL
SCIENCE?

208 *some prolific researchers faked data*: "Does Psychology Need SWaG? The
Ethics of Naturalistic Experiments," *Discover*, January 21, 2018, www
.discovermagazine.com/the-sciences/does-psychology-need-swag-the
-ethics-of-naturalistic-experiments.

208 *and that the famed psychologists*: Susannah Cahalan, *The Great Pretender:
The Undercover Mission That Changed Our Understanding of Madness*
(New York: Grand Central Publishing, 2020); Andrew M. Colman et
al., "A Role in Auditing Hans Eysenck?," *Psychologist* 32 (September
2019), thepsychologist.bps.org.uk/volume-32/september-2019/role
-auditing-hans-eysenck.

208 *And it's not just critics*: Thibault Le Texier, "Debunking the Stanford Prison

Experiment," PsyArXiv, August 8, 2019, doi:10.1037/amp0000401; Gina Perry, *Behind the Shock Machine: The Untold Story of the Notorious Milgram Psychology Experiments* (New York: The New Press, 2013).

208 *brain training for older folks*: David Moreau, Brooke N. Macnamara, and Zach Hambrick, "Overstating the Role of Environmental Factors in Success: A Cautionary Note," PsyArXiv, psyarxiv.com/sv9pz/.

208 *implicit bias training programs*: Patrick S. Forscher et al., "A Meta-analysis of Procedures to Change Implicit Measures," PsyArXiv, August 9, 2019, psyarxiv.com/dv8tu/.

208 *teaching to learning styles*: Harold Pashler et al., "Learning Styles: Concepts and Evidence," *Psychological Science in the Public Interest* 9, no. 3 (2008), doi.org/10.1111/j.1539-6053.2009.01038.x.

209 *The problem is that certain other findings*: Lee Jussim and Kent D. Harber, "Teacher Expectations and Self-Fulfilling Prophecies: Knowns and Unknowns, Resolved and Unresolved Controversies," *Personality and Social Psychology Review* 9, no. 2 (2005), doi.org/10.1207/s15327957pspr0902_3; Joseph P. Simmons and Uri Simonsohn, "Power Posing: P-Curving the Evidence," *Psychological Science* 28, no. 5 (2017), doi.org/10.1177/0956797616658563; M. S. Hagger et al., "A Multilab Preregistered Replication of the Ego-Depletion Effect," *Perspectives on Psychological Science* 11, no. 4 (2016): 546–73, doi:10.1177/1745691616652873; Ulrich Schimmack and Yue Chen, "The Power of the Pen Paradigm: A Replicability Analysis," *Replicability-Index* (blog), September 4, 2017, replicationindex.com/2017/09/04/the-power-of-the-pen-paradigm-a-replicability-analysis/; David Myers, "Is Seasonal Affective Disorder a Folk Myth?," *Talk Psych* (blog), October 18, 2016, community.macmillanlearning.com/t5/talk-psych-blog/is-seasonal-affective-disorder-a-folk-myth/ba-p/5567.

209 *Moreover, the magnitude and reliability*: Paulette C. Flore and Jelte M. Wicherts, "Does Stereotype Threat Influence Performance of Girls in Stereotyped Domains? A Meta-analysis," *Journal of School Psychology* 53, no. 1 (2015): 25–44, doi.org/10.1016/j.jsp.2014.10.002; Moreau, Macnamara, and Hambrick, "Overstating the Role of Environmental Factors in Success"; Tyler W. Watts, Greg Duncan, and Haonan Quan, "Revisiting the Marshmallow Test: A Conceptual Replication Investigating Links Between Early Delay of Gratification and Later

Outcomes," *Psychological Science* 29, no. 7 (2018), doi.org/10.1177 /0956797618761661; "Reversals in Psychology," *Argmin Gravitas*, January 26, 2020, www.gleech.org/psych.

209 *As one former psychology student*: J. Sully (@sullyj3), Twitter, June 29, 2021, 12:39 p.m., twitter.com/sullyj3/status/1409914412815708162.

210 *One of my favorite but contested experiments*: Abigail A. Marsh, Shawn A. Rhoads, and Rebecca M. Ryan, "A Multi-semester Classroom Demonstration Yields Evidence in Support of the Facial Feedback Effect," *Emotion* 19, no. 8 (2019): 1500–1504, doi.org/10.1037/emo0000532.

210 *And stepping back to look*: Brian A. Nosek et al., "Replicability, Robustness, and Reproducibility in Psychological Science," PsyArXiv (2021), psyarxiv.com/ksfvq/.

211 *Let's encourage critical thinking*: Olga Stavrova and Daniel Ehlebracht, "The Cynical Genius Illusion: Exploring and Debunking Lay Beliefs About Cynicism and Competence," *Personality and Social Psychology Bulletin* 45, no. 2 (2018): 254–69, doi:10.1177/0146167218783195.

ACKNOWLEDGMENTS

My profound gratitude flows first to my fellow psychological scientists, of whose insights and creative research I am a cub reporter. They are the smart ones. In my texts and in this little book, I aim to be their publicist—to help spread their gifts to the world, and thereby to increase human rationality, self-understanding, and compassion.

My thanks also flow to those whose guidance has made this a better book than I alone could have written.

At Hope College, my poet-colleague and writing coach, Jack Ridl, helped shape the voice, and the playful spirit, that I hope you have found in these pages.

Christine Brune, my extraordinary Macmillan Learning/Worth Publishers editor for thirty-five years—surely one of the most enduring and rewarding editor/author relationships in American publishing—first inspired me to consider new ways to reframe the best of psychological science for the general public. Macmillan's senior executive program manager Carlise Stembridge has been a similarly wonderful encourager and friend.

Each of these essays passed first through the sensitive mind of Kathryn Brownson, who has worked alongside me for the past quarter century—gathering information, editing, managing projects, and sharing my sense of purpose. Words fall short of expressing what I owe her.

With the support of Macmillan Learning, most essays have also benefited from the painstaking attention of Nancy Fleming, Trish Morgan, or Danielle Slevens. I am privileged to have the support of many excellent editors over half a century of writing. But I've known none more gifted than these three. Each has been so painstaking, so constructive, so creative— and so encouraging.

With combined intelligence and diligence, Jackson Parrott crafted the endnotes.

This book exists thanks to the initiative of my agent, John Brockman, who immediately grasped the vision and shared it with his friends at the Macmillan trade companies. Brockman Inc. (including Max Brockman and Russell Weinberger) is a gift to its authors.

Eric Chinski, Farrar, Straus and Giroux's vice president and editor in chief, affirmed the idea, and soon handed the ball to the executive vice president for editorial development, Will Schwalbe, who has, on behalf of Farrar, Straus and Giroux, mentored this book's evolution. Under Will's guiding hand, and also thanks to the deft touches of assistant editor Samantha Zukergood, essays have been winnowed, new essays have been created, and individual essays have been sharpened, expanded, or pruned. Ingrid Sterner then skillfully finessed the manuscript and meticulously fine-tuned the copious endnotes. The end result is, indeed, a better book than I could have written alone. The pack is greater than the wolf.

A NOTE ABOUT THE AUTHOR

David G. Myers is a social psychologist and professor of psychology at Hope College. His articles have appeared in dozens of scientific periodicals and magazines, from *Science* to *Scientific American*. He is also the author of seventeen books, including psychology's most widely read textbook, which has sold more than eight million copies worldwide. Myers resides in Holland, Michigan.